PENCIL SKETCHING

THOMAS C. WANG

to my parents......

Library of Congress Catalog Card Number 77-1095
ISBN 0-442-29177-9

Designed by Thomas C. Wang

Published in 1977 by Van Nostrand Reinhold Company Inc.
135 West 50th Street. New York. N.Y. 10020 U.S.A.

Van Nostrand Reinhold Australia Pty. Limited
480 Latrobe Street. Melbourne, Victoria 3000. Australia

Van Nostrand Reinhold Company Limited
Molly Millars Lane, Wokingham. Berkshire. RG11 2PY. England

16 15 14 13 12 11

Library of Congress Cataloging in Publication data

Wang, Thomas C.
Pencil sketching

Bibliography: p
Includes index
1. Pencil drawing. I. Title
NC890.W25 741.214 77-1095
ISBN 0-442-29177-9

TABLE OF CONTENTS

Wang '76

In this book, my main concern has been to present the fundamental principles of pencil sketching as simply as possible so that the layman and student can learn to sketch and draw with pencil.

Pencil is often seen as a cheap graphic medium. To a lot of students, pencil sketching is less interesting to learn because of its messiness and the lack of colors. It is true that pencil has its faults and limitations, yet it is still the most widely used tool for artists today.

Pencil is also inexpensive in terms of the paper and other materials that are required. These materials are easy to carry and there is no lengthy or difficult preparation involved. The pencil medium is highly flexible, and it is responsive to any variation of pressure or direction applied to it. this allows the artist to produce various kinds of strokes as well as a wide spectrum of tone, ranging from light gray to intense black; this could all be done with one simple sketching pencil. Unlike other media that require time to dry, sketching with pencil is far less time-consuming. The pencil can be used independently as a finishing medium, and it can also be combined with many other media as outline or touch-up.

Very often the pencil is the easiest medium to get used to, due to our familiarity with it in daily use, as in writing. This kind of familiarity is very helpful in teaching pencil-sketching techniques because the students are free to concentrate on other problems which make learning to sketch easier. I also find pencil sketching the most appropriate medium for expressing the many characteristics of natural environments. The expression of natural form and texture with pencil can be made rich and complex in ways that neither pen nor color markers can achieve.

It is my hope that this book will not only express the amazing potential of the pencil but also will increase the student's ability to sketch rapidly and confidently with pencil.

Thomas Chi-chung Wang

Dec. 1976, Urbana, Illinois.

TYPES OF PENCIL SKETCHING

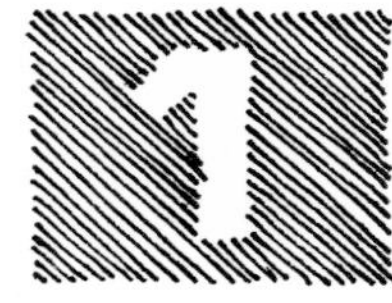

OUTLINE DRAWING (layout)

Building form mechanical;
simple; no detail;
unfinished.

QUICK SKETCH

use only a few lines to
express the image;
a finished sketch by itself.

LINE DRAWING

Line width similar;
no variations;
shows details.

SHADING

Use a variety of tones
to express different
levels of planes.

FINISHED RENDERING

Carefully detailed;
well proportioned;
accurate perspective.

IMAGE STUDY

sketchy ; quick ;
lacks details

EQUIPMENT

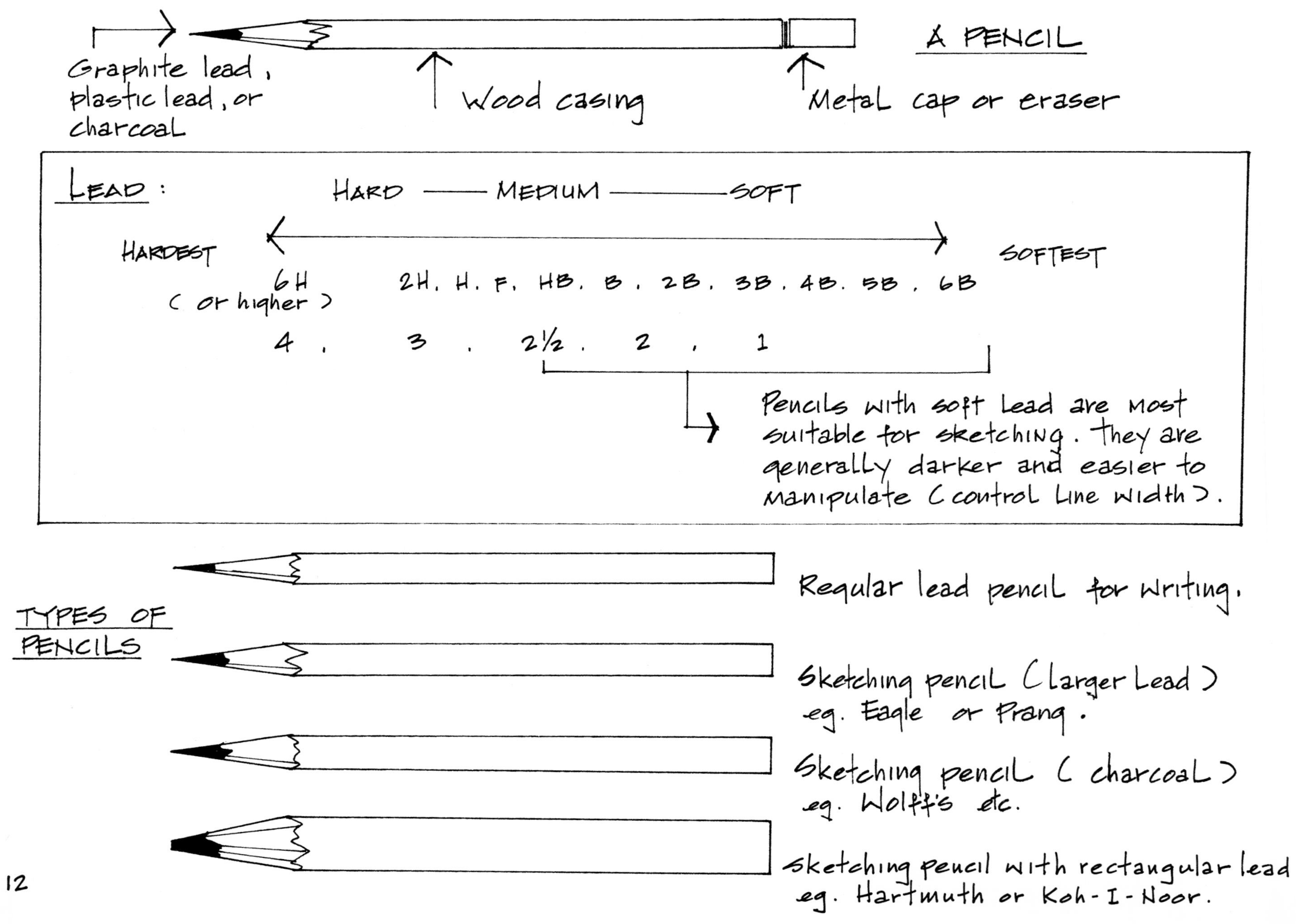

A PENCIL
Graphite lead, plastic lead, or charcoal
Wood casing
Metal cap or eraser
LEAD:
HARD —— MEDIUM —— SOFT
HARDEST
SOFTEST
6H (or higher)
2H. H. F. HB. B. 2B. 3B. 4B. 5B. 6B
4. 3. 2½. 2. 1
Pencils with soft lead are most suitable for sketching. They are generally darker and easier to manipulate (control line width).
TYPES OF PENCILS
Regular lead pencil for writing.
Sketching pencil (Larger Lead) eg. Eagle or Prang.
Sketching pencil (charcoal) eg. Wolff's etc.
sketching pencil with rectangular lead eg. Hartmuth or Koh-I-Noor.

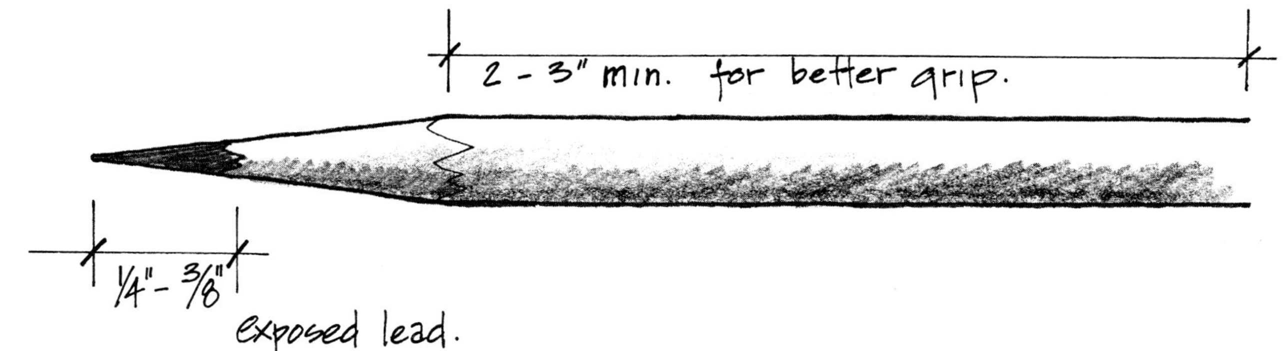

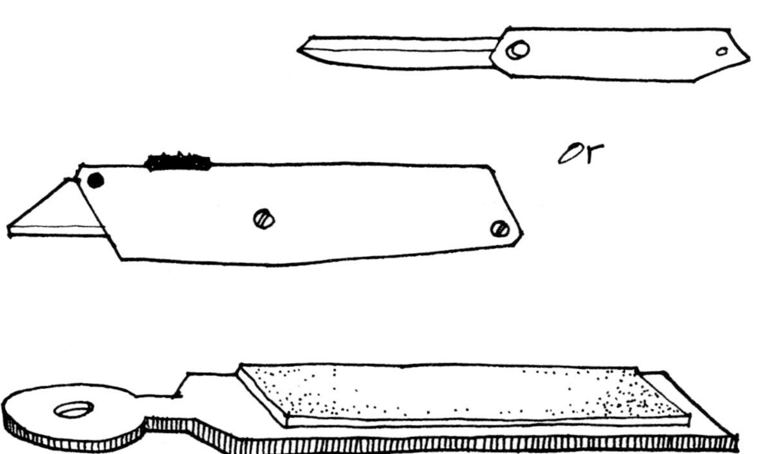

Sharpen your pencil with a pencil sharpener or a small pocket knife.

Use long exposed side of the lead for better shading. Use sides of the exposed lead for broad strokes.

Avoid pointed or conical tip except in drawing details. A sharp lead point will scratch the paper and hinder movement.

Rotate the pencil to maintain a consistent lead point.

Use a sanding block for fine sharpening.

3 PAPERS

Generally, softer pencils are recommended for smooth papers and harder pencils for coarser or rough papers.

Coarse papers tend to wear out the points of pencils. Therefore, they are more difficult to use in sketching because of the accumulation of fine graphite particles.

Rough papers are not reccommended for small-scale drawings because the texture cannot reveal the fine details.

PAPERS

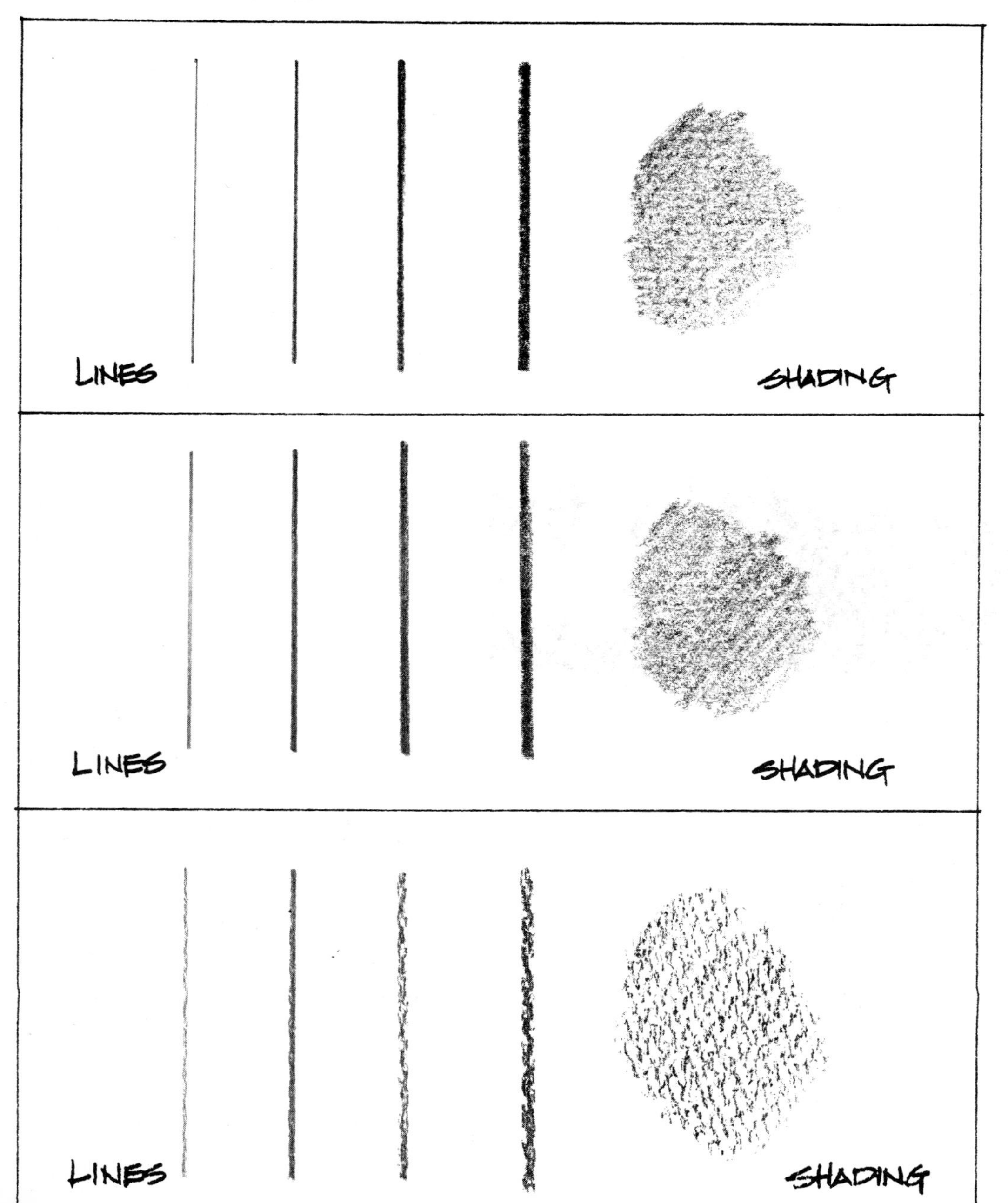

EXAMPLE: 1 Regular bonded paper.

Excellent line quality. and even shading.

EXAMPLE: 2 Strathmore Alexis Drawing 400-3.

Excellent line quality but shading slightly grainy.

EXAMPLE: 3 Strathmore Water-color 400 series.

A unique paper for sketching; texture coarse and grainy; lines lack crispiness & sharpness.

EXAMPLE A: on Strathmore Alexis drawing 400-3

A high-quality paper for pencil sketching. Its surface is smooth yet non oily.

EXAMPLE B: on Strathmore Watercolor Paper 400 Series

A thick & coarse paper primarily for watercolor. It is best suited for large-format drawings in pencil sketching. It is not suitable for details and outline.
Not recommended for beginners!

TECHNIQUES

INCORRECT: WRITING FORM

CORRECT: SKETCHING FORM

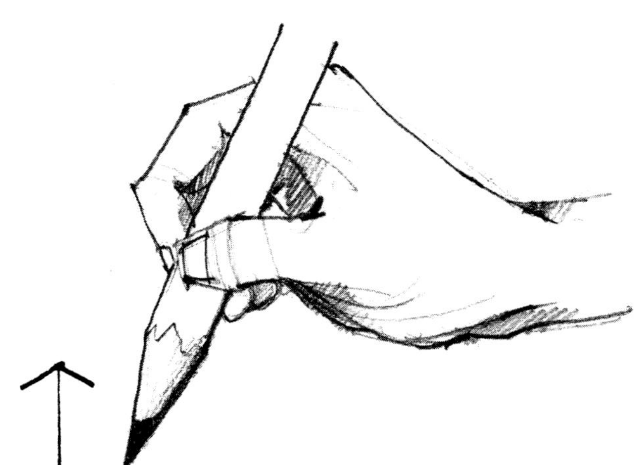

Minimum wrist motion; mostly finger movement. It is less flexible because the grip is too tight. This form is not recommended for sketching except for detailing.

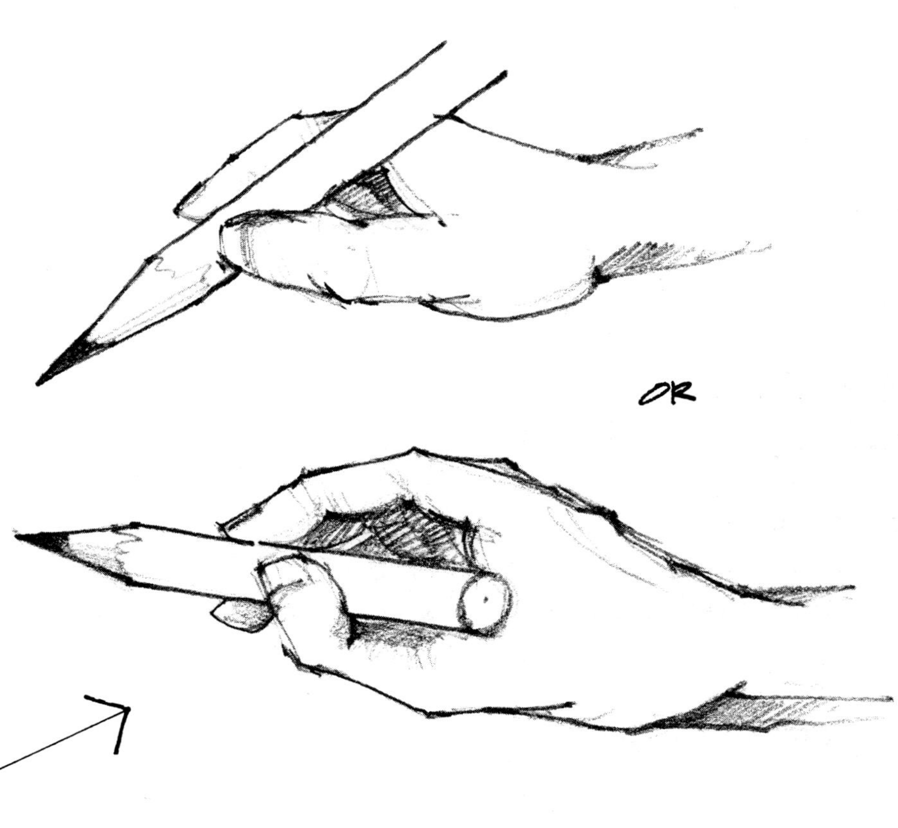

Maximum wrist motion; larger arc; covers more area. Loose grip for better line control; it is easier to manipulate the pencil.

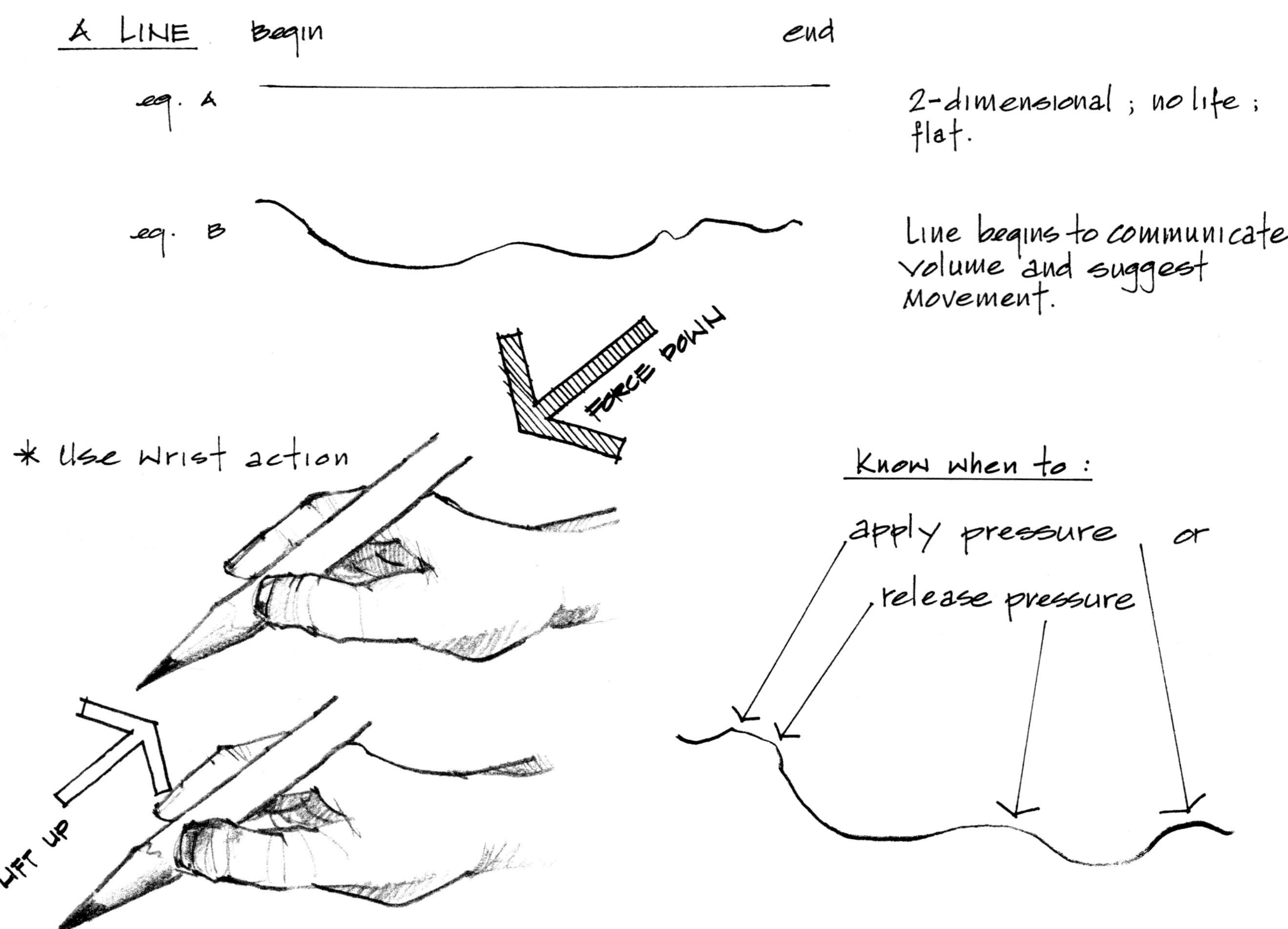
A LINE
begin
end
eg. A
2-dimensional ; no life ; flat.
eg. B
Line begins to communicate volume and suggest movement.
FORCE DOWN
* Use wrist action
Know when to :
apply pressure
or
release pressure
LIFT UP

LINE

DIRECT LINE

Consistent line weight shows confidence and the use of arm or wrist motion.

SKETCHY LINE

Inconsistent line weight indicates a lack of confidence : afraid to make mistakes and uses too many short strokes (a result of finger movements).

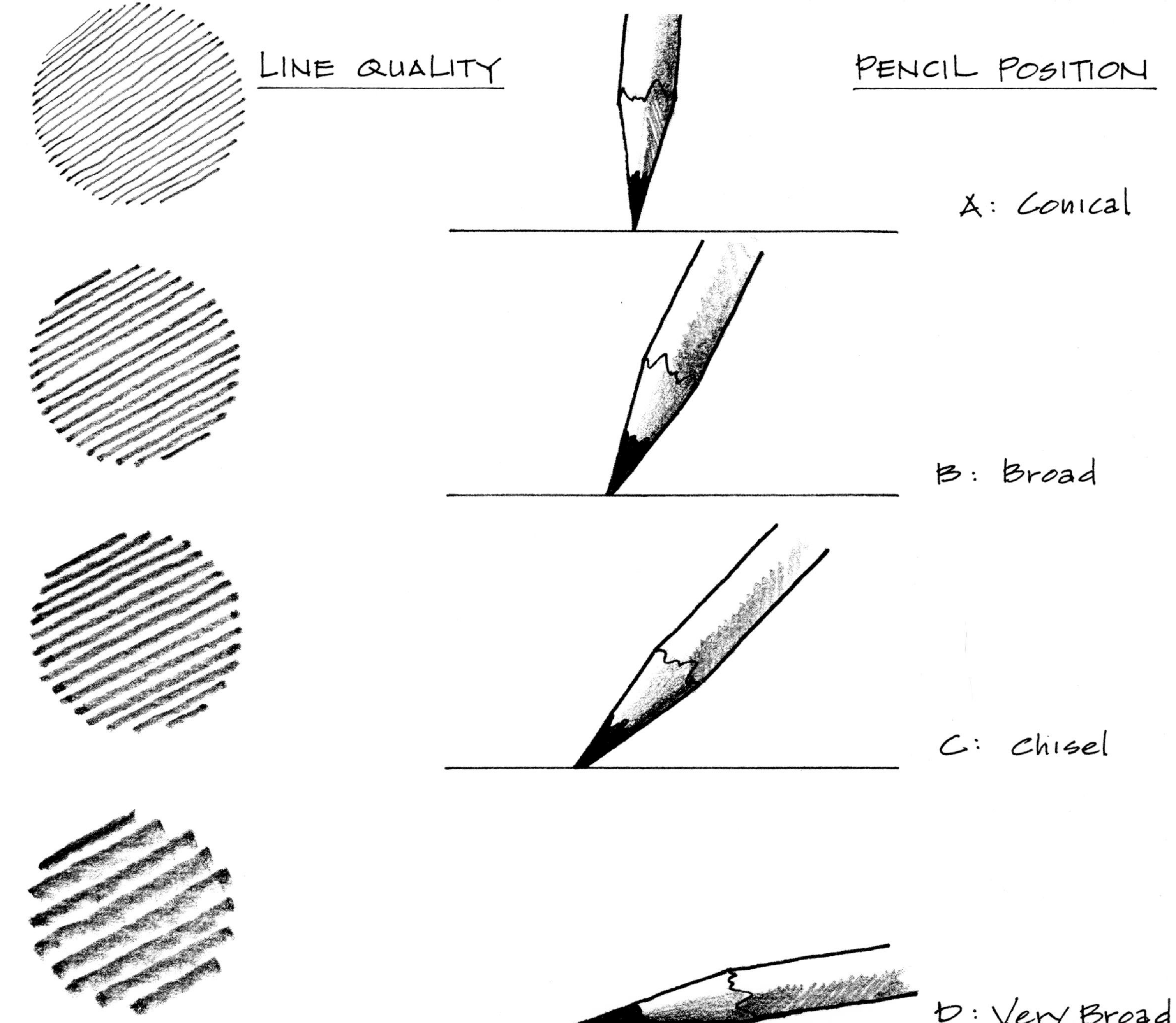
LINE QUALITY
PENCIL POSITION
A: Conical
B: Broad
C: Chisel
D: Very Broad

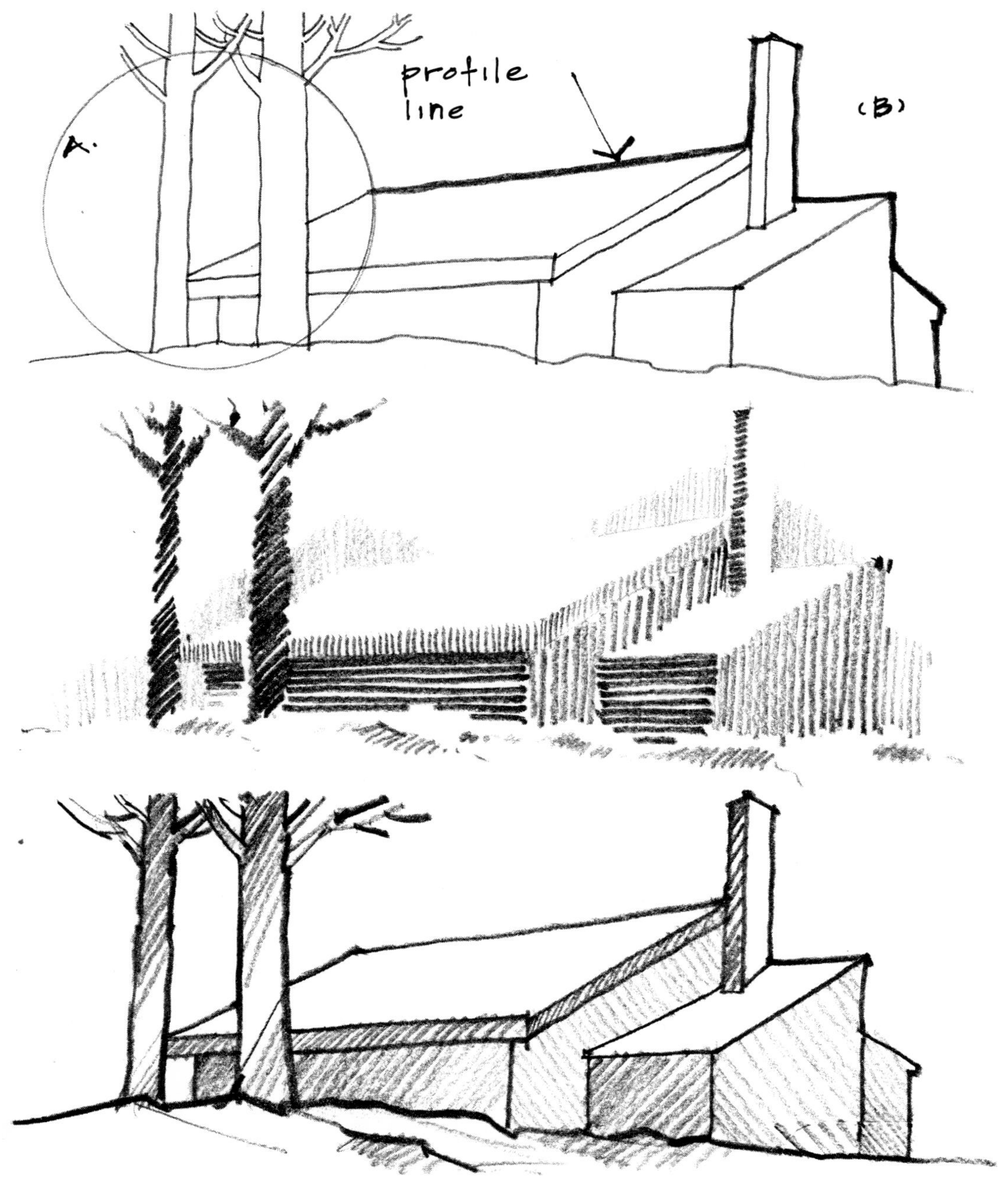

A: Line drawing

B: Line drawing with profile to differentiate background and foreground.

Use line of tone to indicate difference in planes (looks like shading).

Line and tone combined.

WITHOUT PROFILE LINE

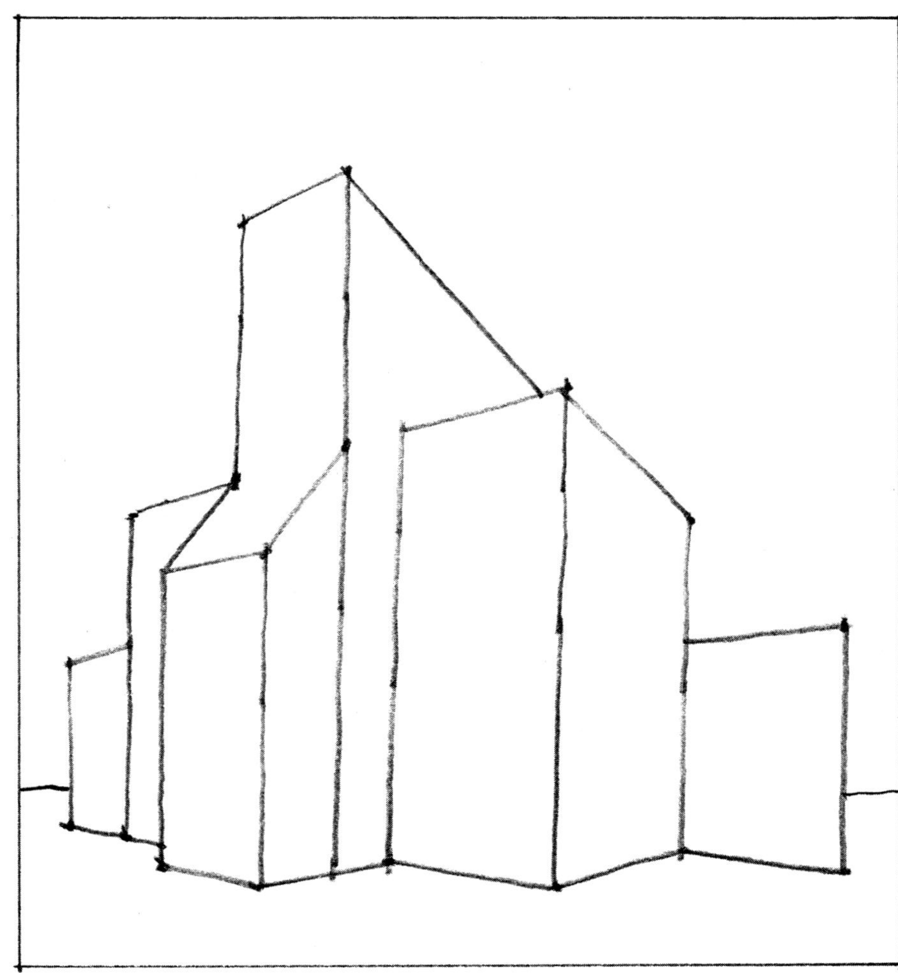

simple line drawing

WITH PROFILE LINE

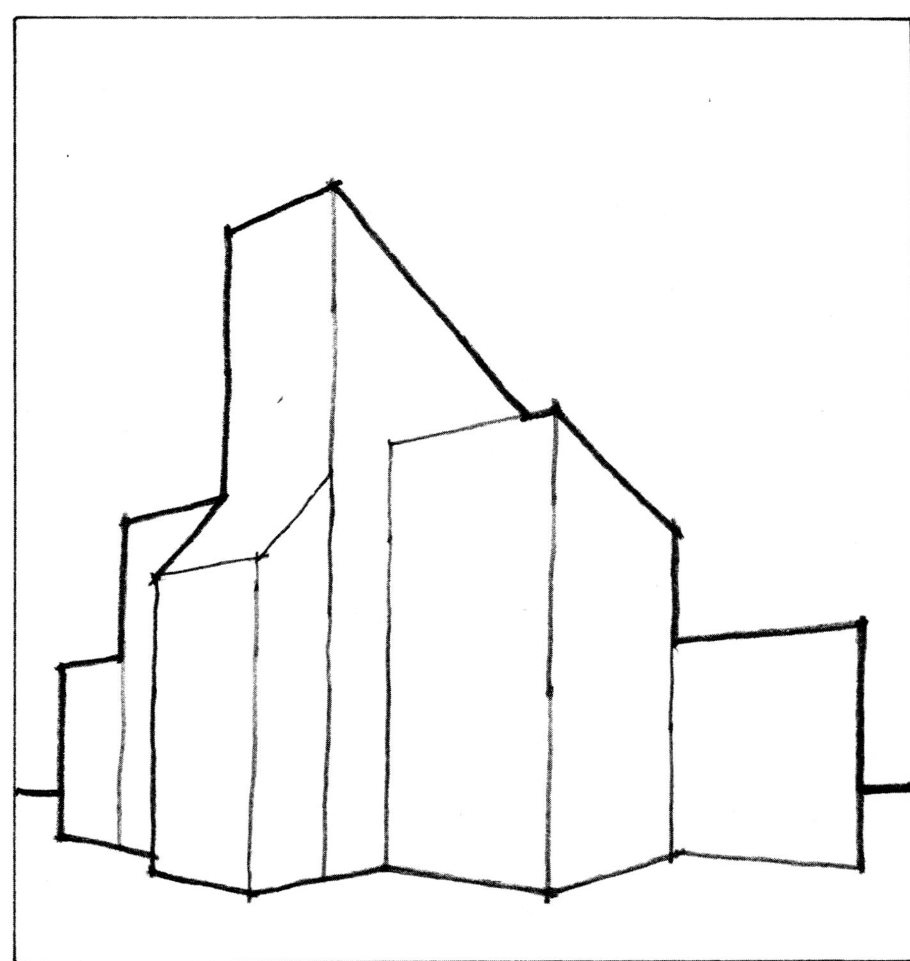

Profile line separates object from background. Object looks more 3-dimensional.

IN this example: different line weights suggest different distances. the drawing becomes more 3-D and has depth.

COMMENTS: flat; dull; no difference in depth.

1: LINE WIDTH SIMILAR

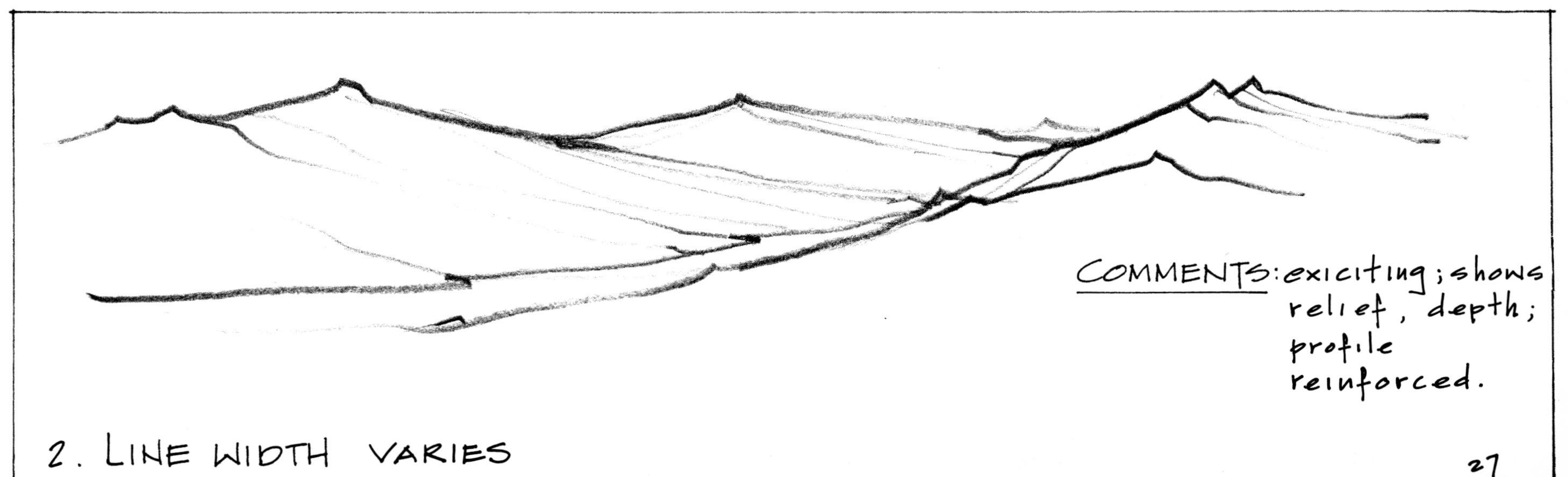

2. LINE WIDTH VARIES

LINE

Lighter line defines background.

thick profile lines define massiveness of buildings and bring them out in front of the background (sky and mountain).

thick profile lines define foreground plant materials (shrubs, tree trunks).

Profile line defferentiates building and ground.

Middle ground — building mass as prime subject.

COMPOSITION

EXAMPLE: Scene of a golf course

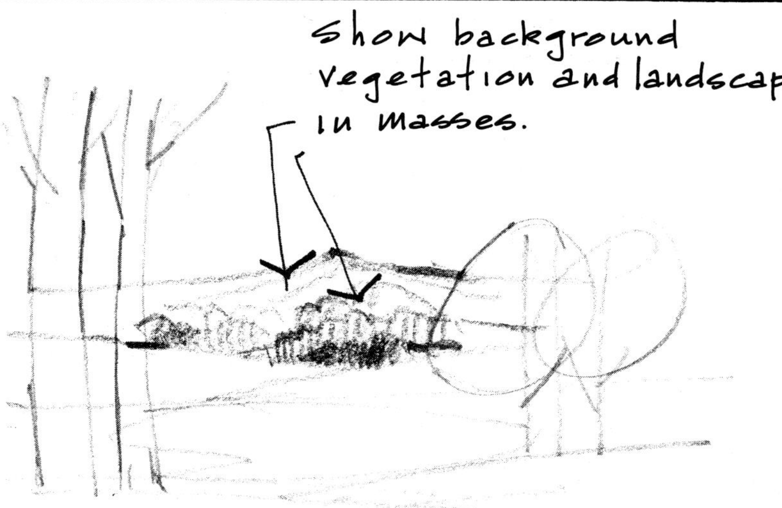

1. Background

3- Foreground
Use as framing; form leads into subject matter;
Mood setting; should have a lot of details and contrast.

2- Middle ground
Usually the theme of the picture; should indicate details.

FOREGROUND MIDDLE GROUND 'theme' BACKGROUND

SHADING

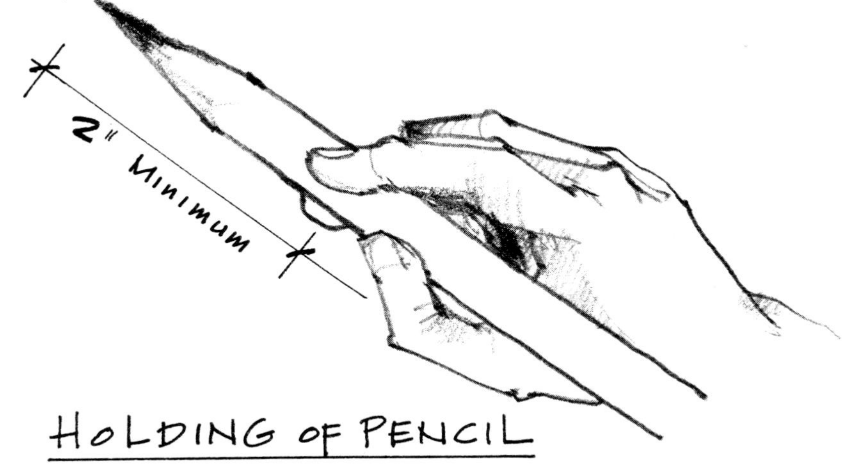

HOLDING OF PENCIL

At least 2" up the tip; relax; use finger or wrist movement.

POSITION OF PENCIL

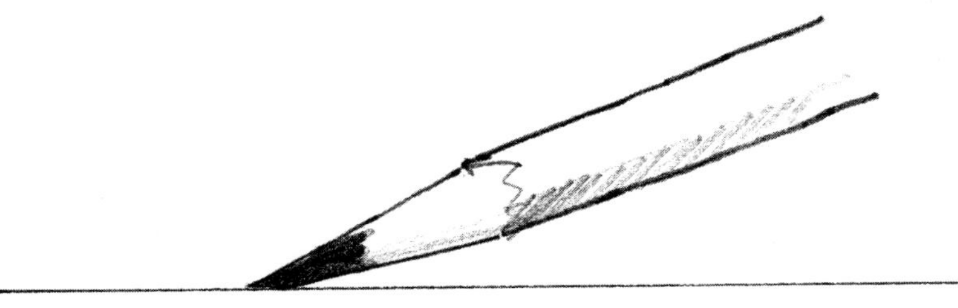

Hold pencil at an angle (e.g. chisel point or broad stroke) Use side of lead tip or broad side of lead for shading

Coarse; revealing texture (pencil strokes).

Smooth (stroke marks disappear)

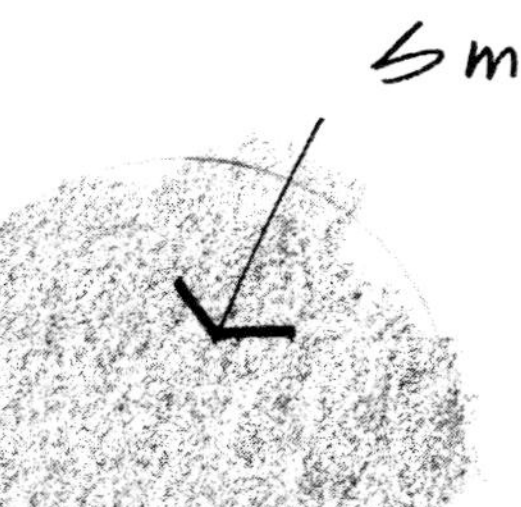

Black, smooth

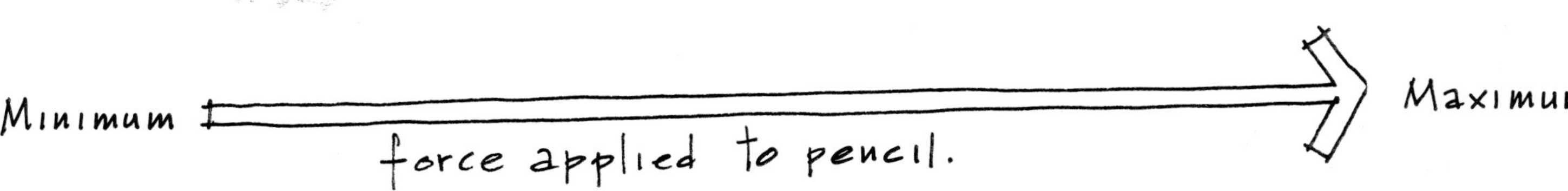

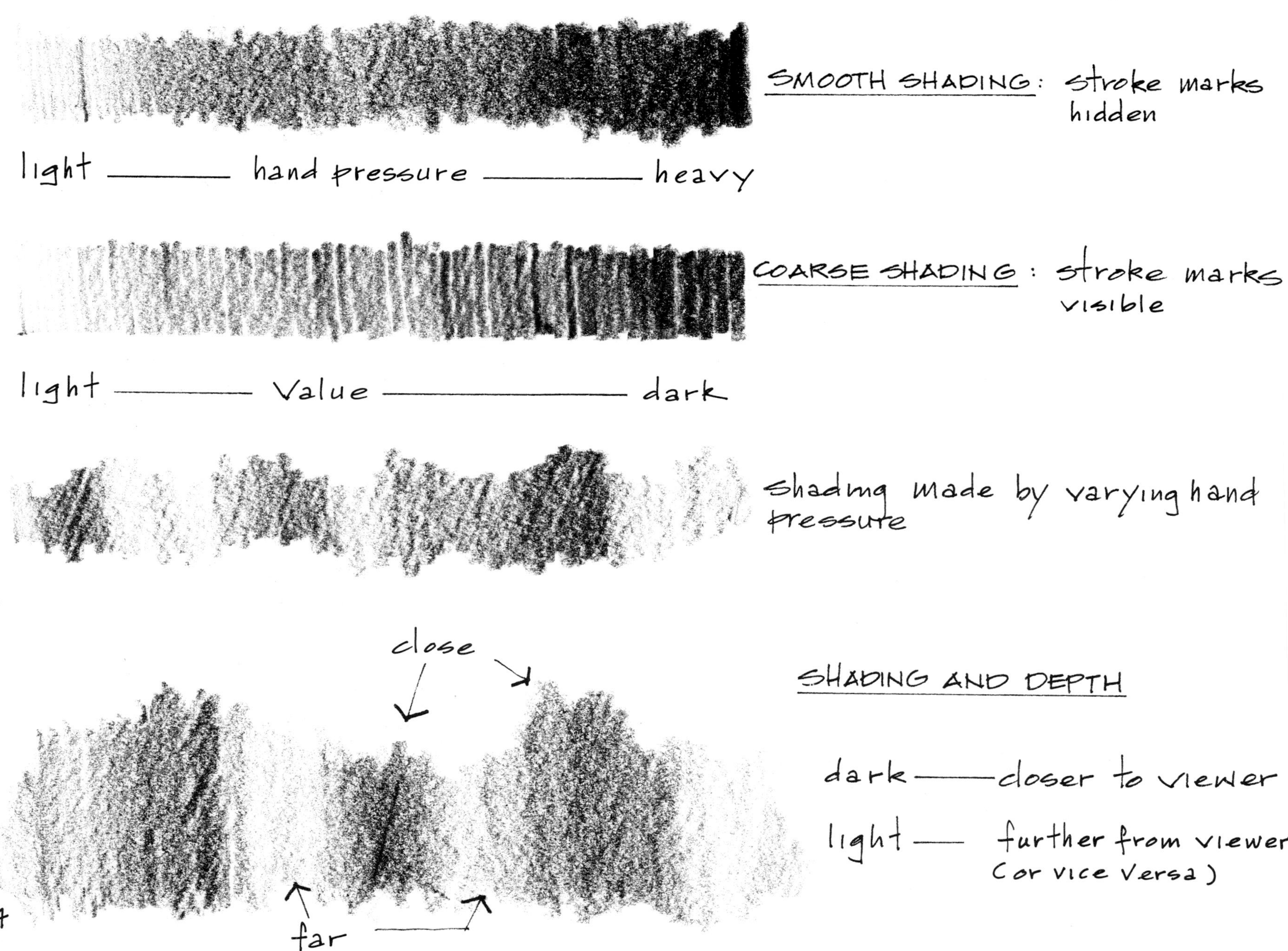
SMOOTH SHADING: stroke marks hidden
light —— hand pressure —— heavy
COARSE SHADING: stroke marks visible
light —— Value —— dark
shading made by varying hand pressure
close
SHADING AND DEPTH
dark —— closer to viewer
light —— further from viewer (or vice versa)
far

IN GENERAL:

Use diagonal strokes to create texture.

Use vertical strokes to shade vertical planes.

Use horizontal strokes to shade horizontal planes.

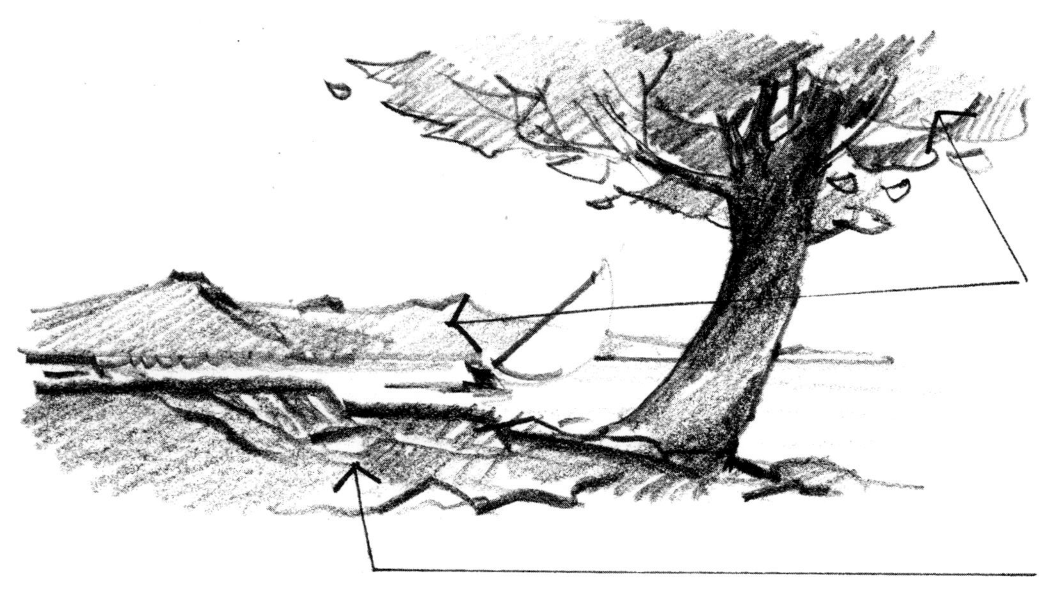

Direction of shading should be consistent.

Stroke direction can vary to reflect the variety of planes (such as rock outcrop in foreground).

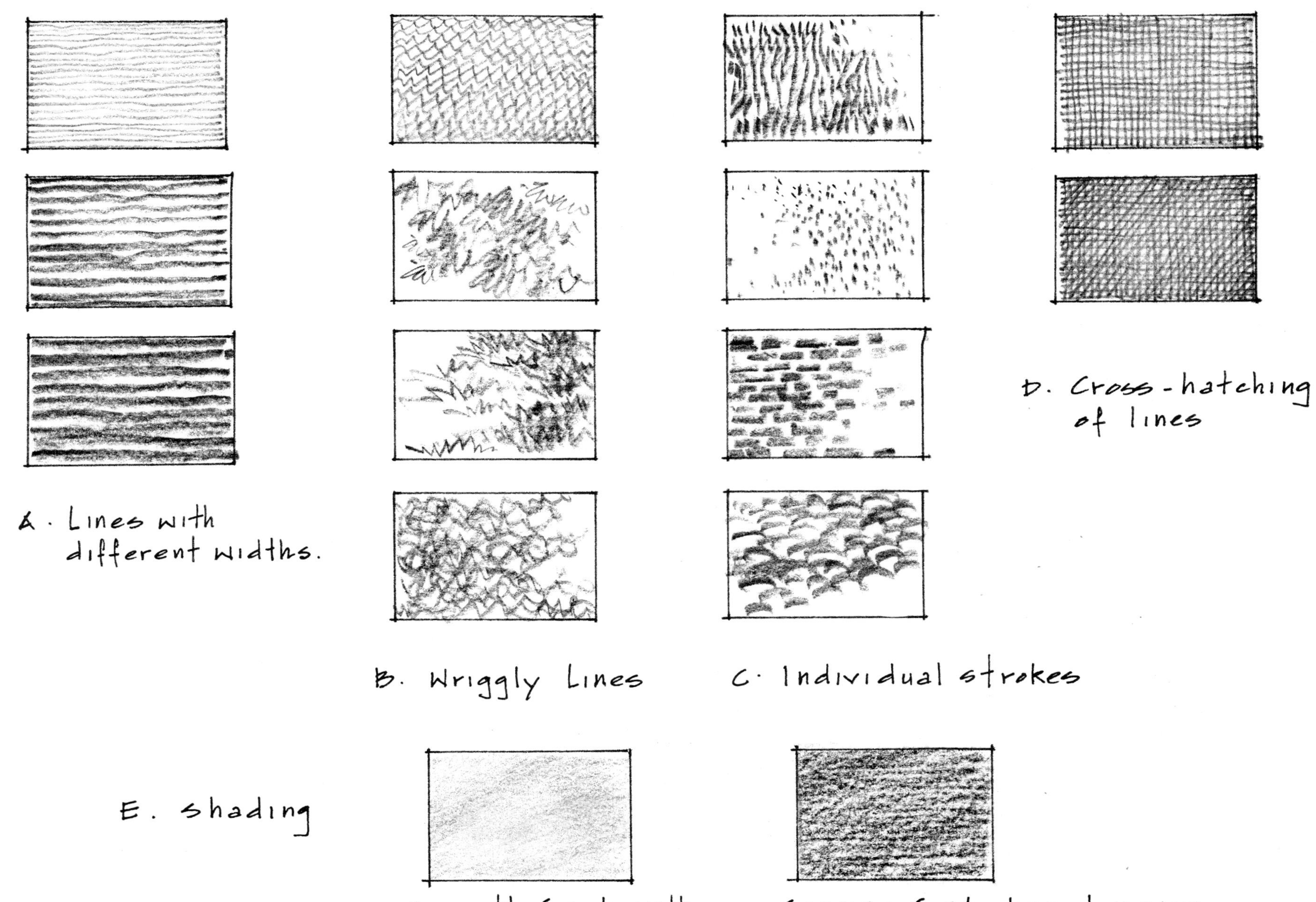
A. Lines with different widths.
B. Wriggly Lines
C. Individual strokes
D. Cross-hatching of lines
E. shading
smooth (rub with cotton ball etc.)
Coarse (shading done on coarse surface)

Line texture
Cross-hatching
Wriggly-line texture
Shading texture

these trees are closer to the viewer. therefore. they don't have to be shown as entire trees.
dark profile line around building
Parts of the tree trunks are not shaded inorder to create depth and contrast against dark background.
Mound in front
darken the center of focus (leads eye Movement).
foreground materials (rocks etc.) should have darker profile lines.

8 LANDFORMS

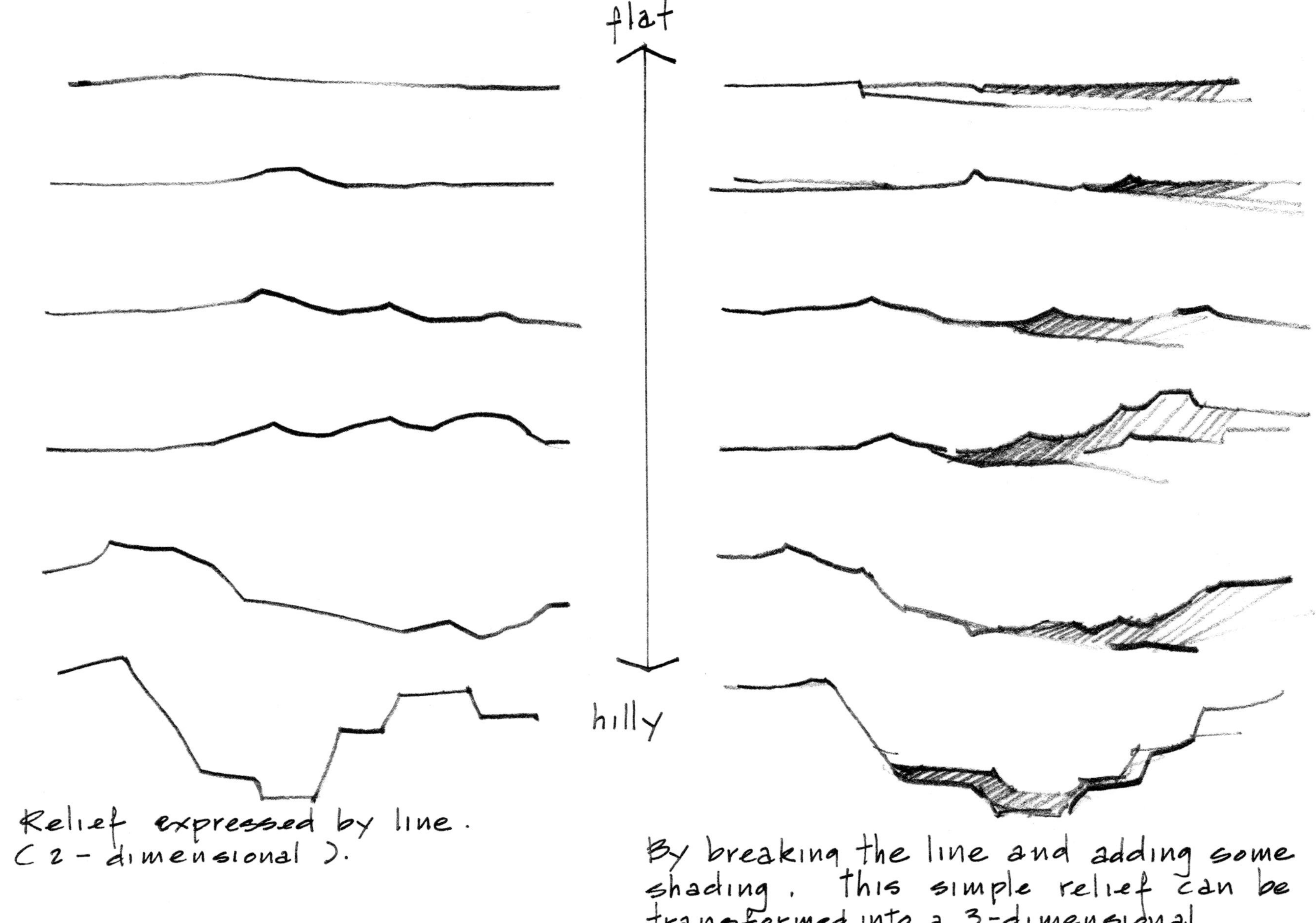

Relief expressed by line. (2-dimensional).

By breaking the line and adding some shading, this simple relief can be transformed into a 3-dimensional landform.

HOW TO DRAW LANDFORMS (1)

step · 1 — one continuous line

step · 2 — break the line into two segments

step · 3 — add shading to indicate depth and change the surfaces

step · 4 — add More lines:
background lines – lighter
foreground lines – darker

add More shading.

step · 5 — Finished !!

step. 1

two lines; begins to show depth.

step. 2

change straight lines into curvilinear lines. this indicates the bending of landform and begins to suggest movement.

step. 3

add shading to indicate depth.

step. 4

darker and heavier foreground lines help to bring out the transition of depth.

step. 5

additional shading and background filling complete the scene.

shading in this case not only suggests depth but also indicates surface materials (smooth/coarse) as well as the change in planes (surfaces).

9 VEGETATION

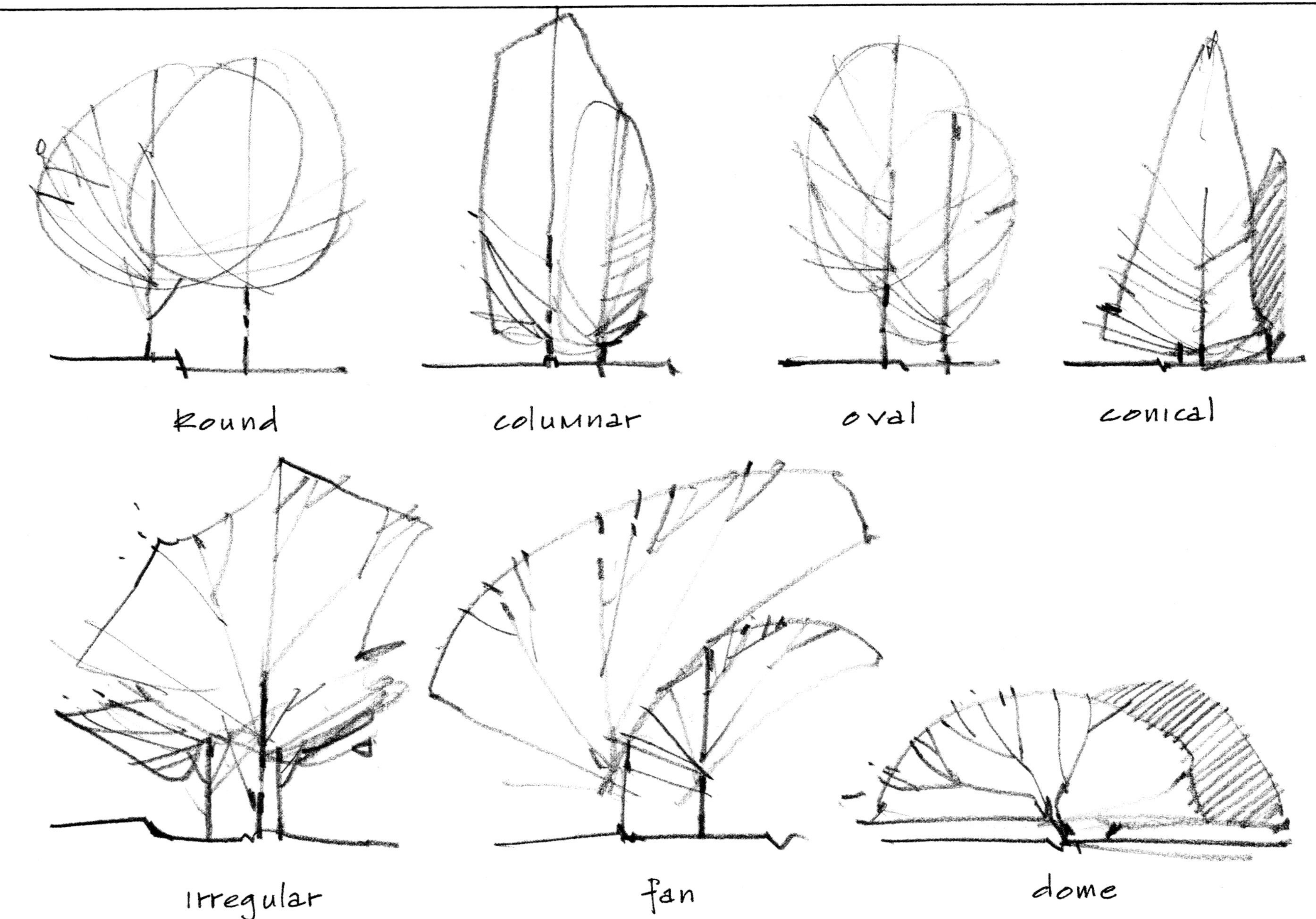
round
columnar
oval
conical
irregular
fan
dome

BASIC SHRUB FORMS

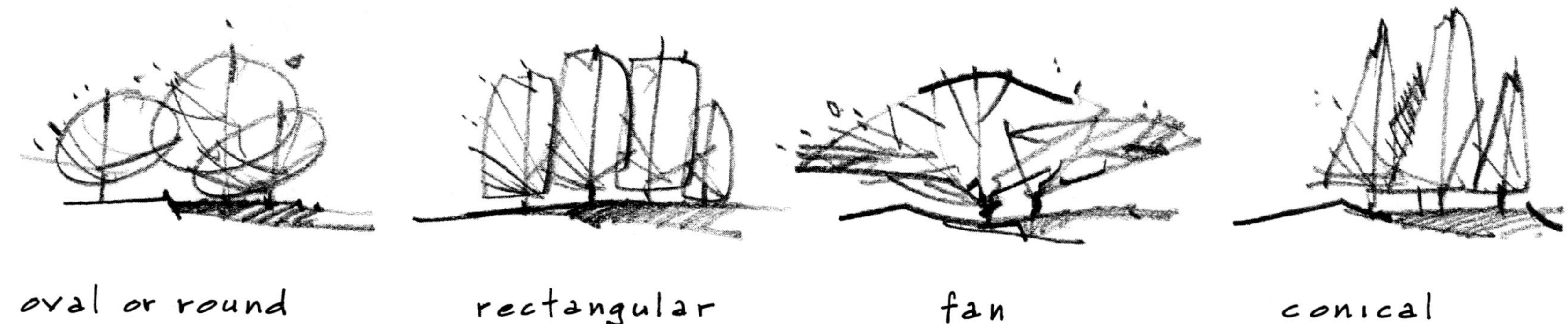

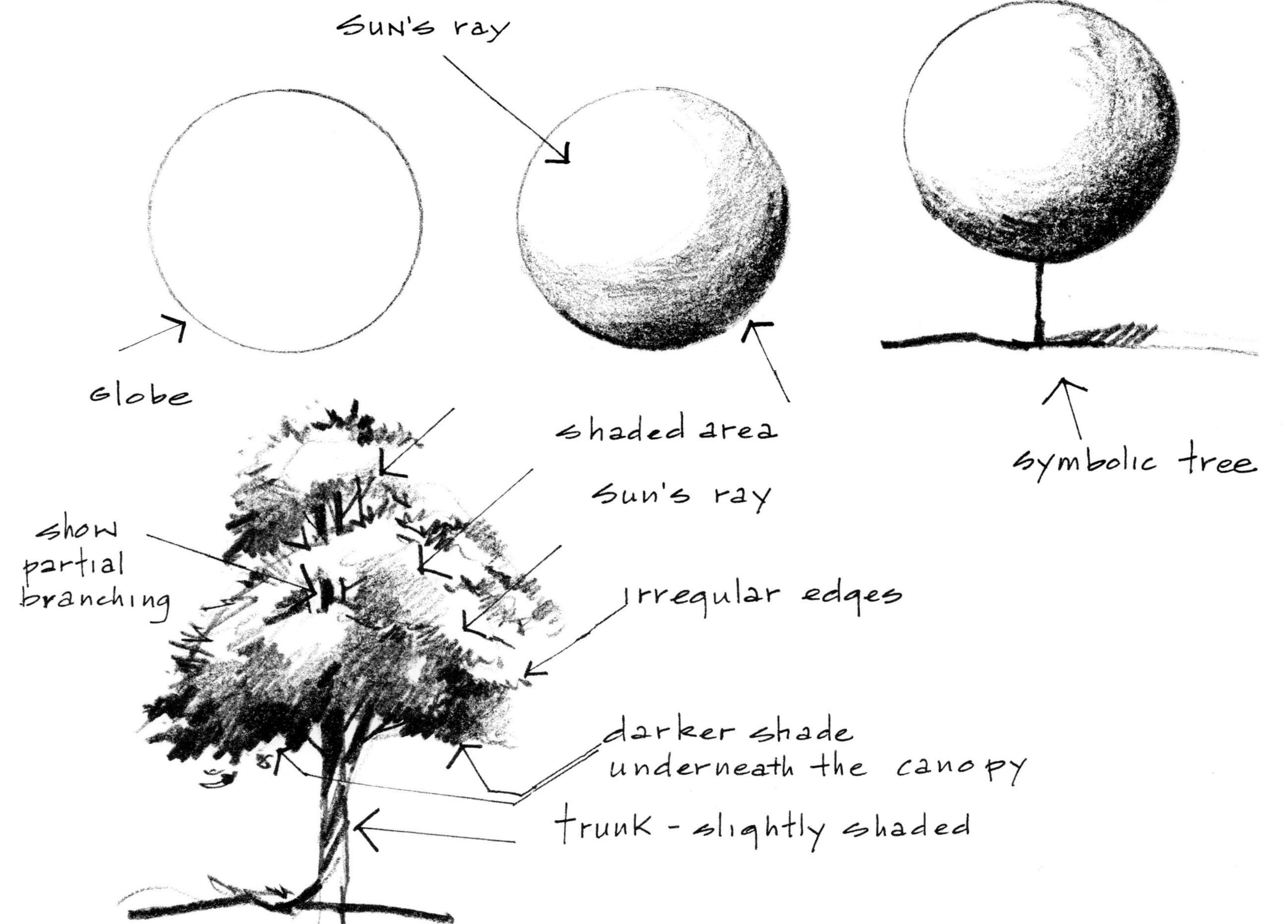
Sun's ray
Globe
shaded area
symbolic tree
Sun's ray
show partial branching
irregular edges
darker shade underneath the canopy
trunk - slightly shaded

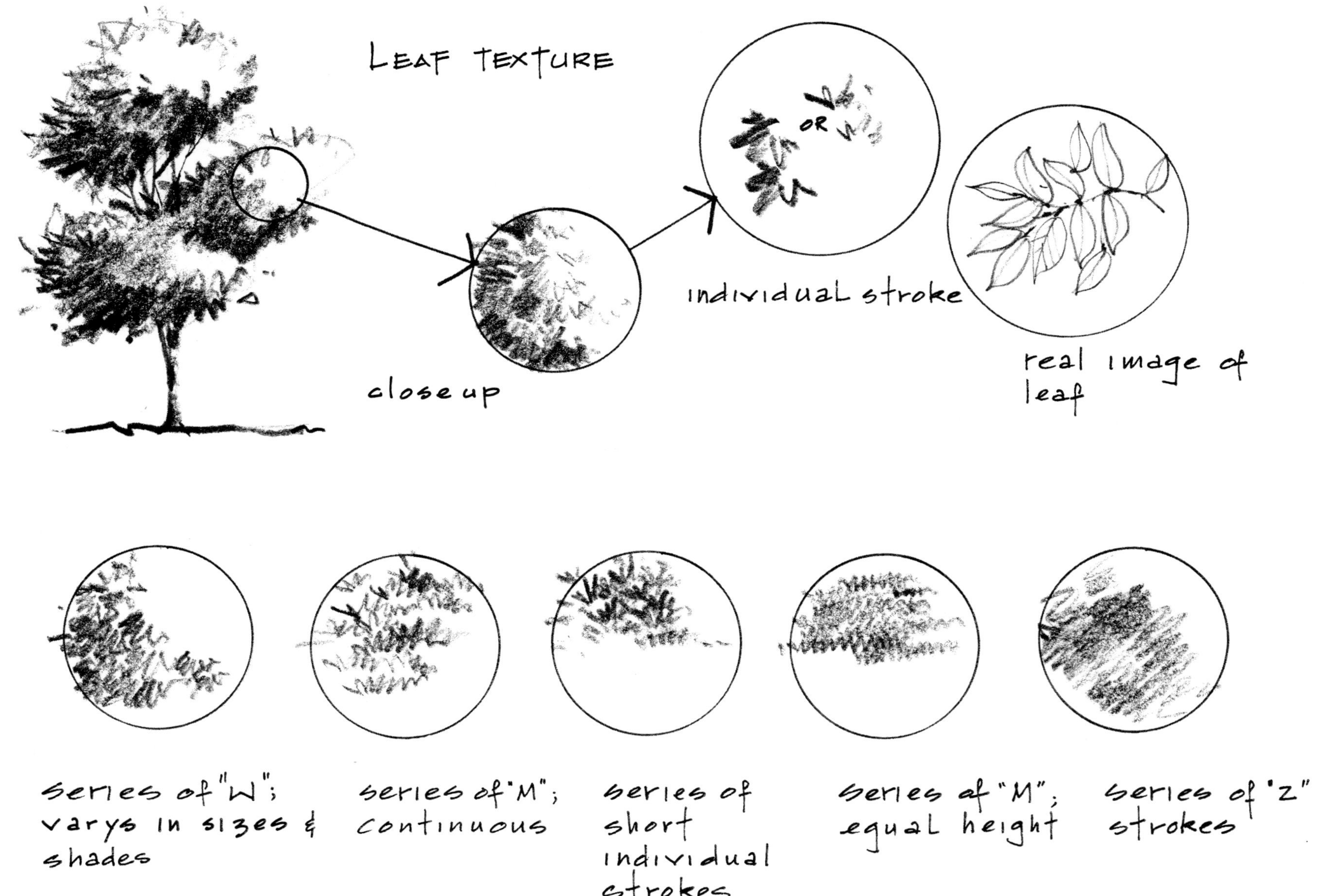
LEAF TEXTURE
OR
individual stroke
close up
real image of leaf
series of "W"; varys in sizes & shades
series of "M"; continuous
series of short individual strokes
series of "M"; equal height
series of "Z" strokes

EVERGREEN TREES

GROUND COVERS

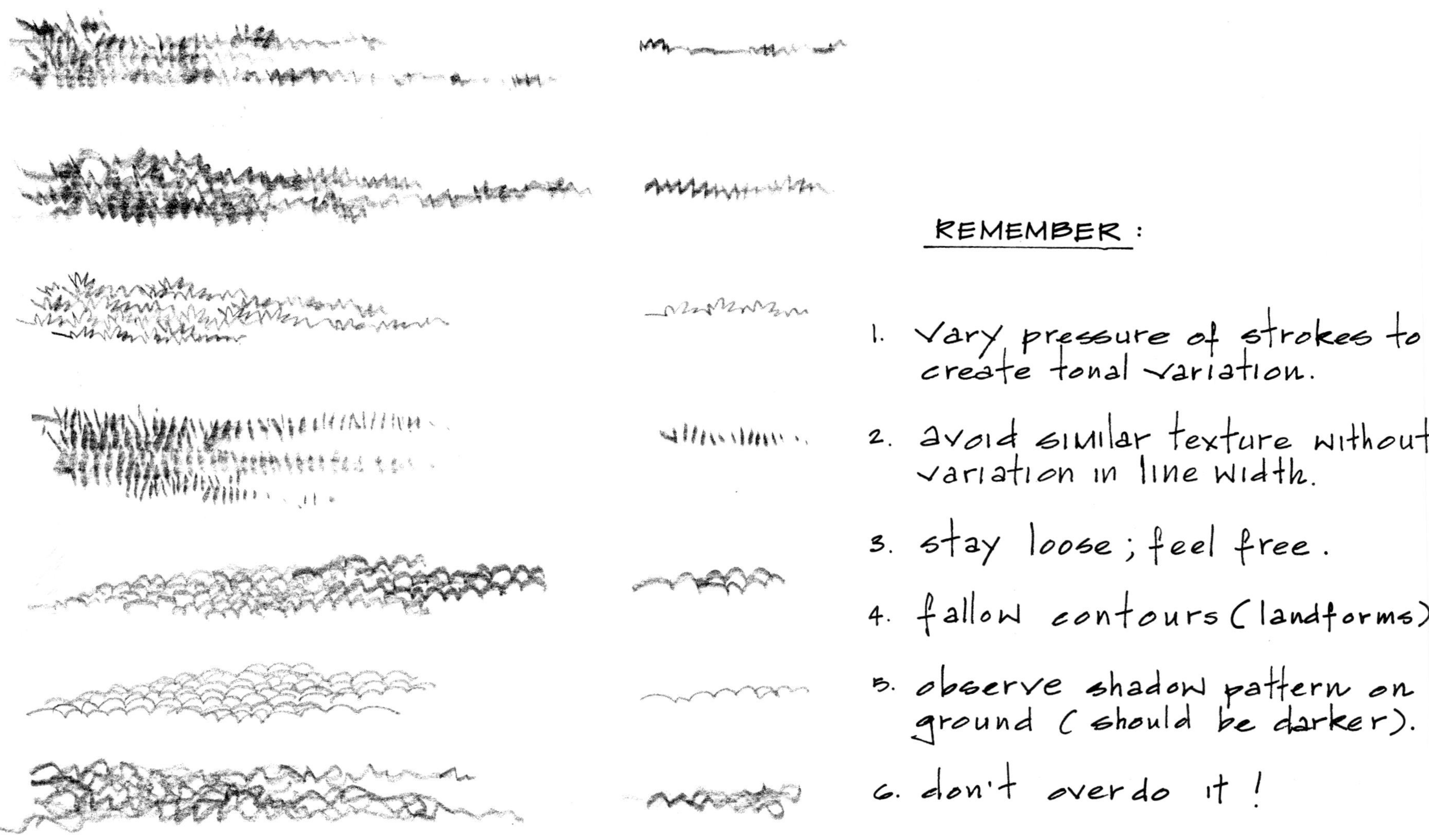

REMEMBER:

1. vary pressure of strokes to create tonal variation.
2. avoid similar texture without variation in line width.
3. stay loose; feel free.
4. fallow contours (landforms).
5. observe shadow pattern on ground (should be darker).
6. don't overdo it!

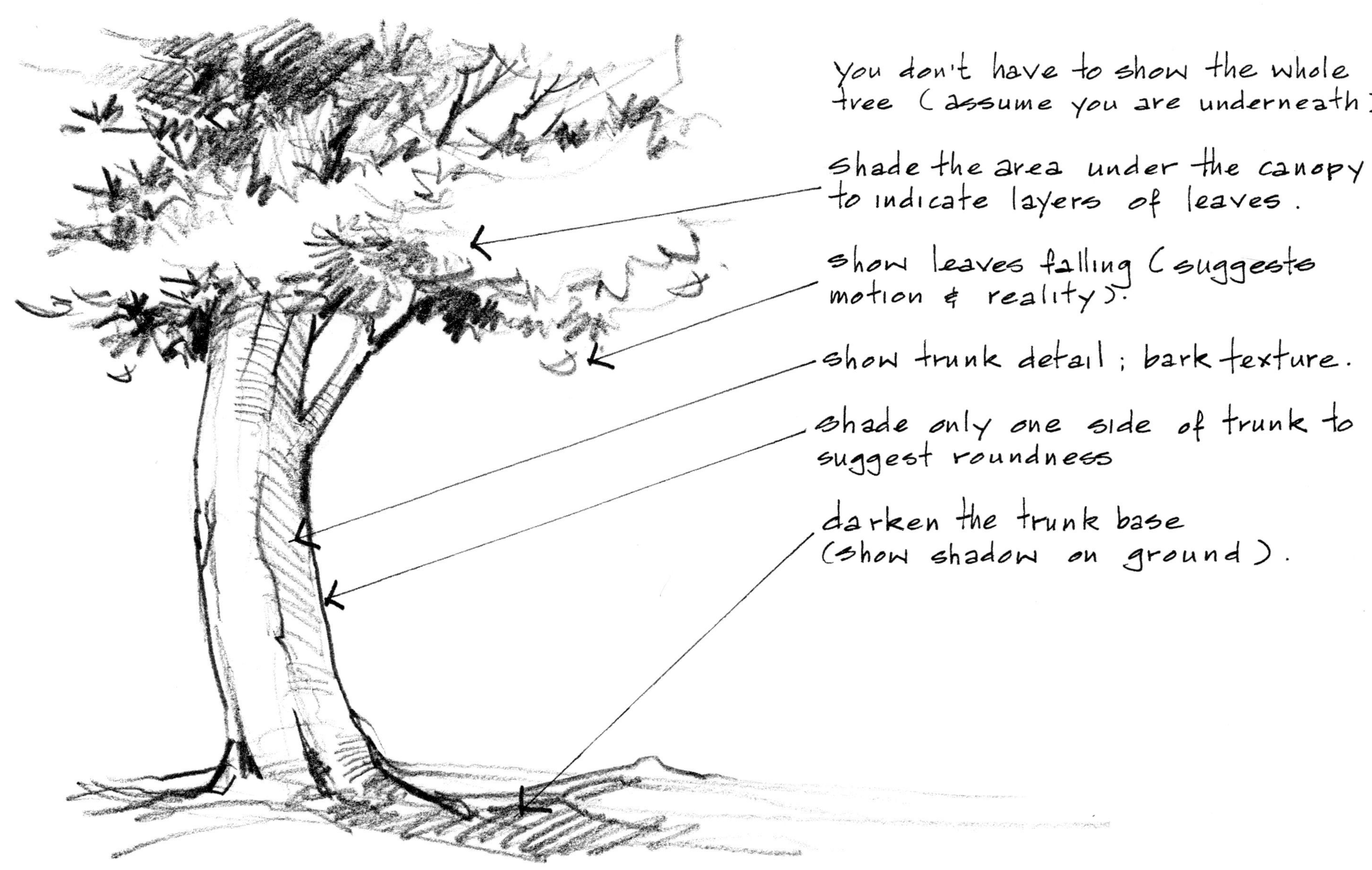
you don't have to show the whole tree (assume you are underneath).
shade the area under the canopy to indicate layers of leaves.
show leaves falling (suggests motion & reality).
show trunk detail; bark texture.
shade only one side of trunk to suggest roundness
darken the trunk base (show shadow on ground).

TREES WITHOUT LEAVES

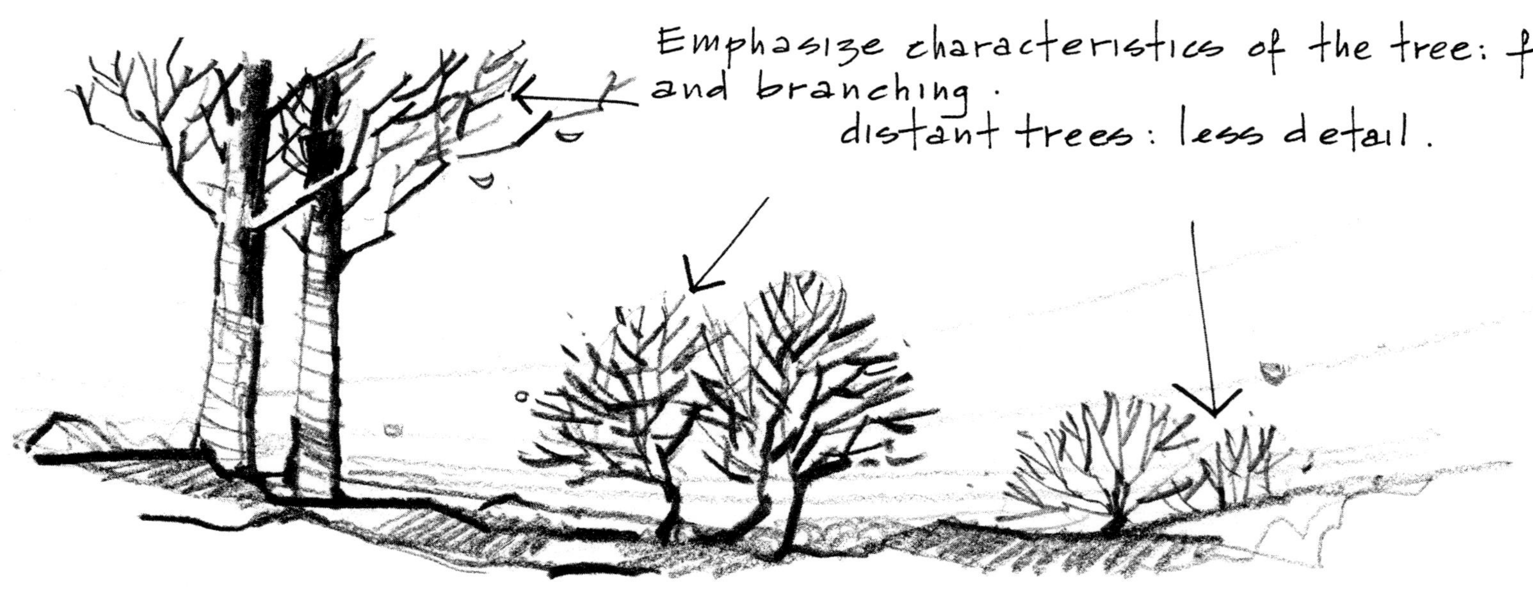

UPRIGHT

HORIZONTAL

DROOPING

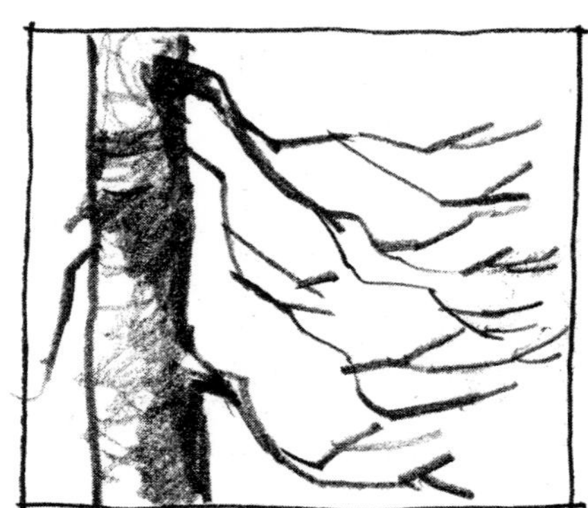

- sketch the basic tree form (outline)

step : 1

sun

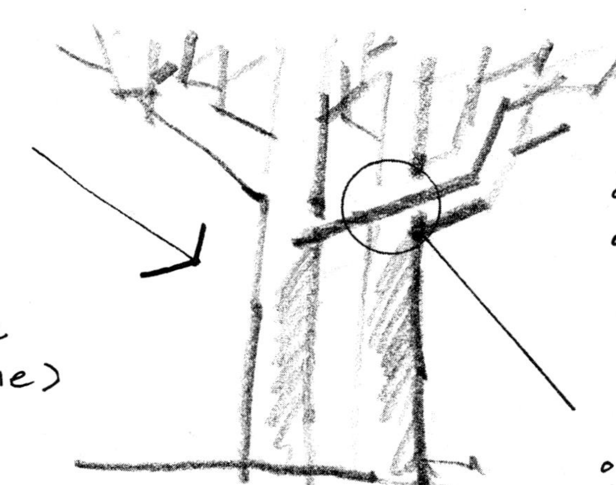

- observe sun's rays.
- use thicker and darker line to outline the shaded side of the trunk.
- leave white areas like this to bring out depth.
- begin shading
- add branches.

step : 2

- refine shading.
- add finer branching by using a sharper pencil.
- darken the bottom of the trunk (ground line).

step : 3

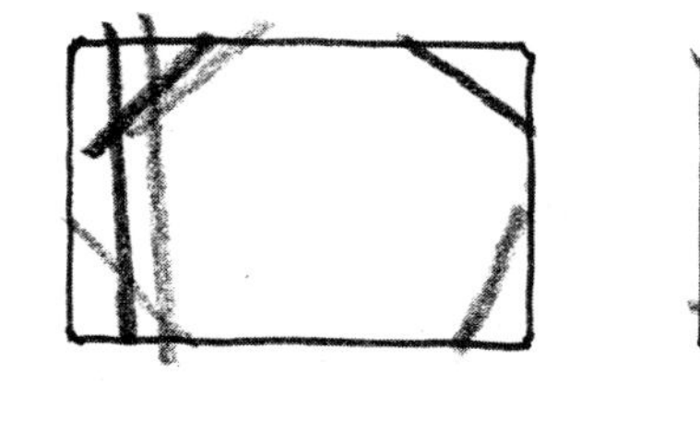

sheet control

balance

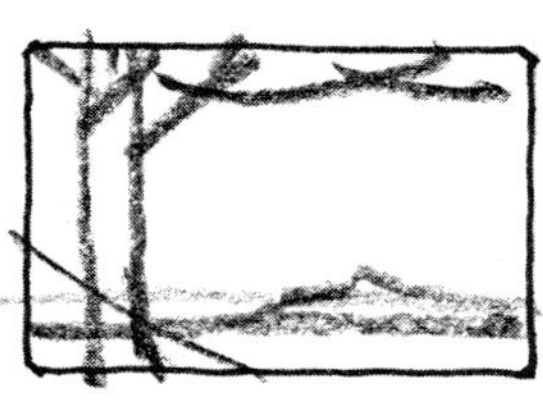

framing

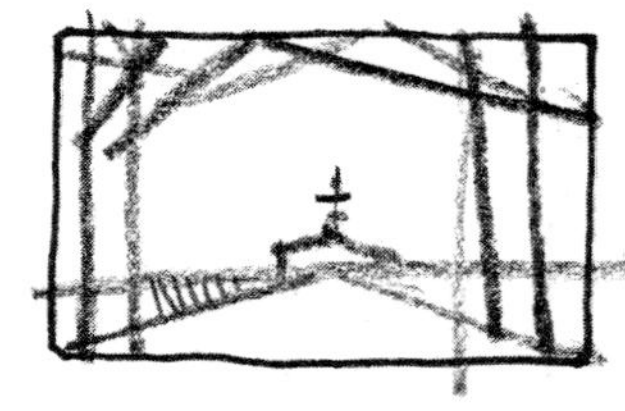

lead into subject matter

light effect

WATER

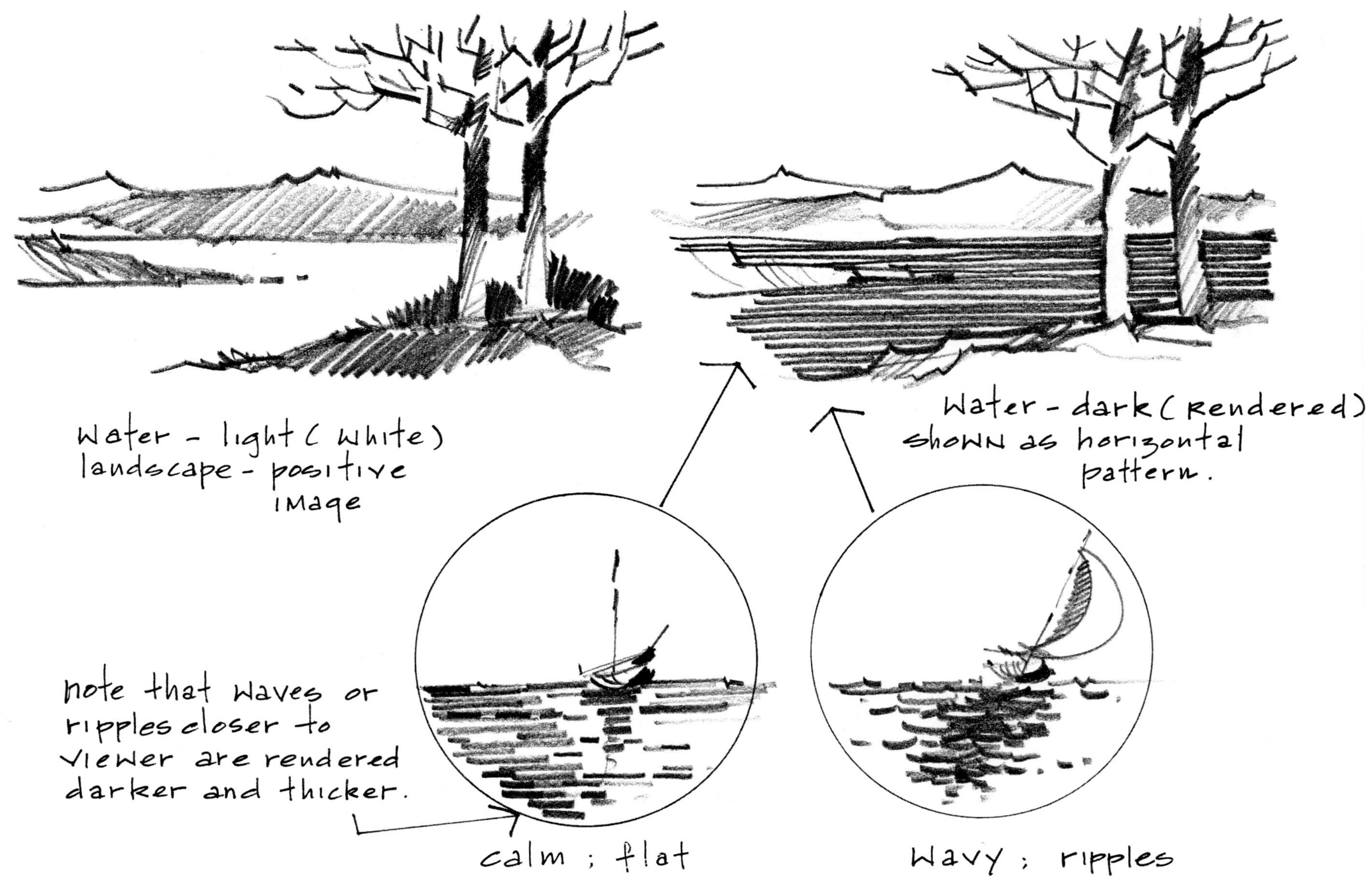
water - light (white)
landscape - positive
image
Water - dark (Rendered)
shown as horizontal
pattern.
note that waves or
ripples closer to
viewer are rendered
darker and thicker.
calm ; flat
wavy ; ripples

Use short strokes to express wavy water; leave white areas to indicate waves.

Use long parallel lines to indicate calm water surface.

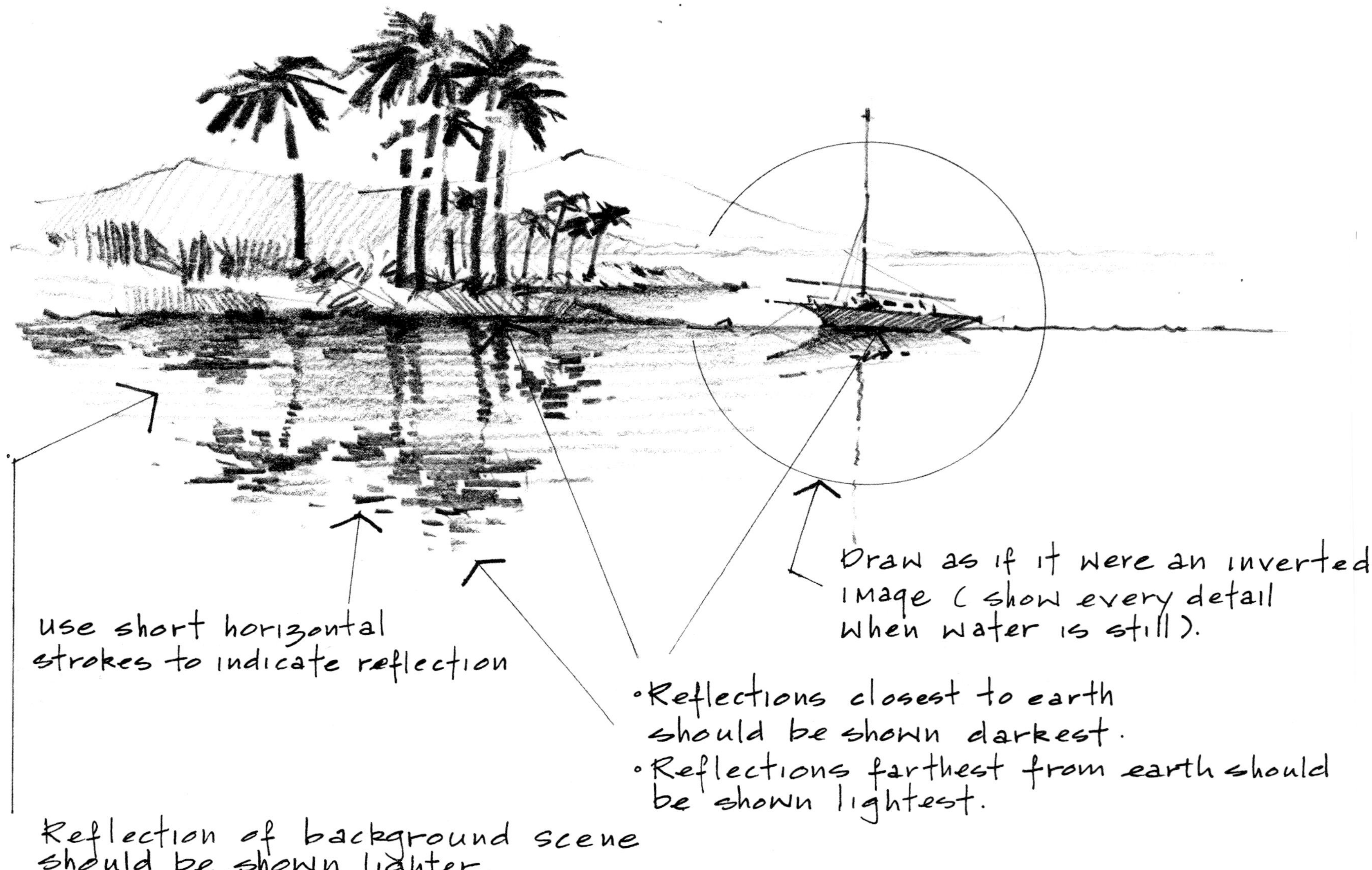
Draw as if it were an inverted image (show every detail when water is still).
Use short horizontal strokes to indicate reflection
•Reflections closest to earth should be shown darkest.
•Reflections farthest from earth should be shown lightest.
Reflection of background scene should be shown lighter.

Reflections of objects on wavy water surface often produce distorted and elongated images.
Use continuous strokes to represent wavy reflection.

SKY

Leave it alone – white

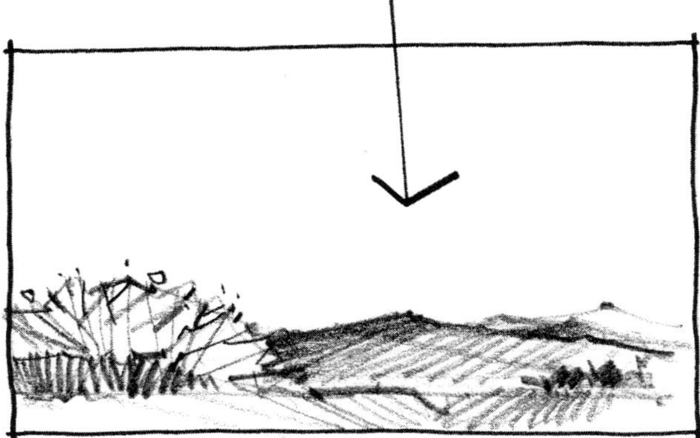

be realistic. show some clouds.

treat it as background – use texture to fill in the openness.

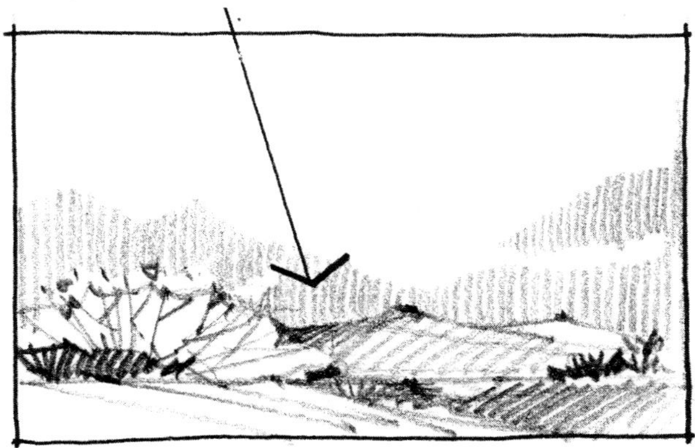

put a few lines across the sky to fill in the void – symbolic.

SKY (EXAMPLE)

SHADE AND SHADOW

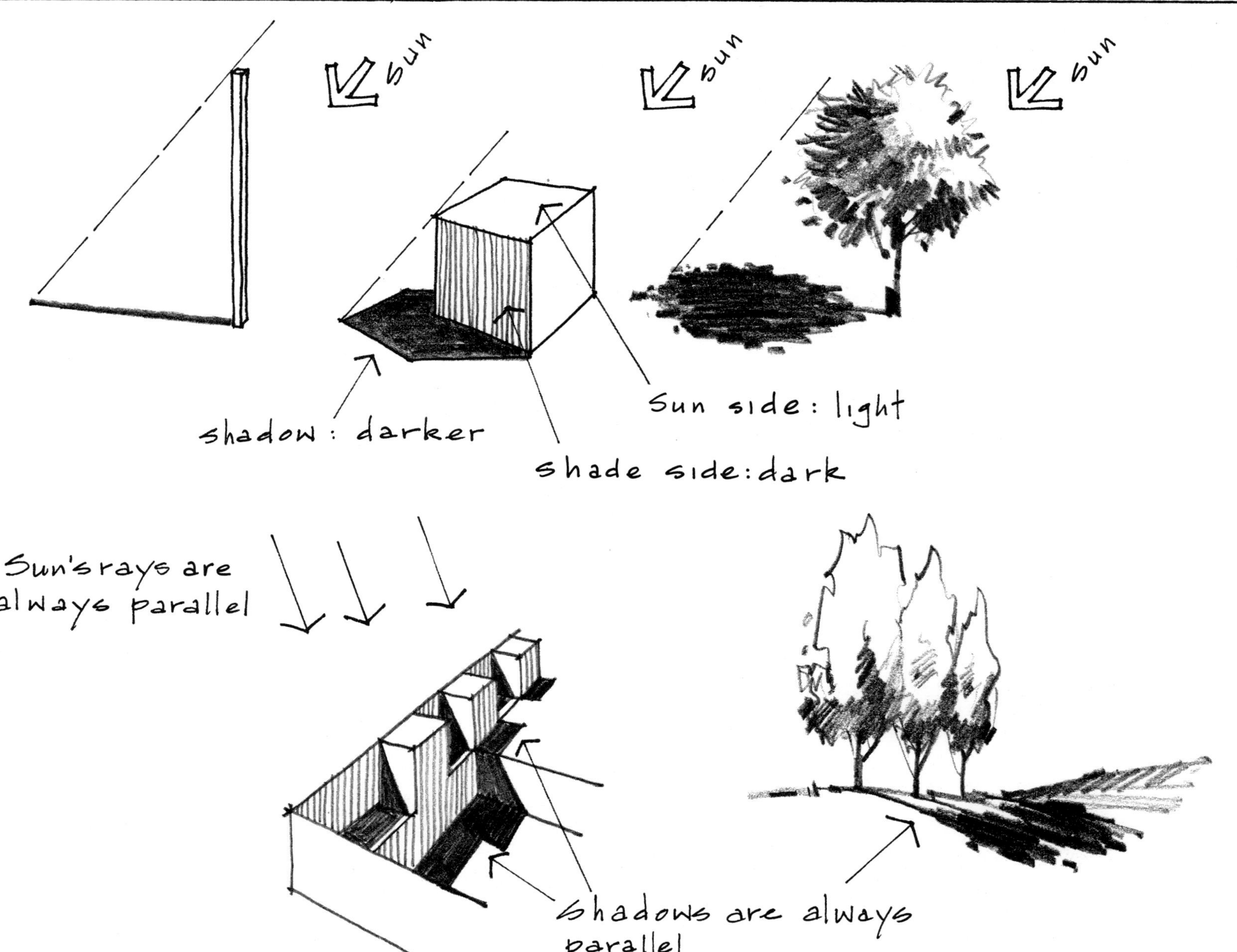
sun
sun
sun
shadow : darker
Sun side : light
shade side : dark
Sun's rays are always parallel
Shadows are always parallel

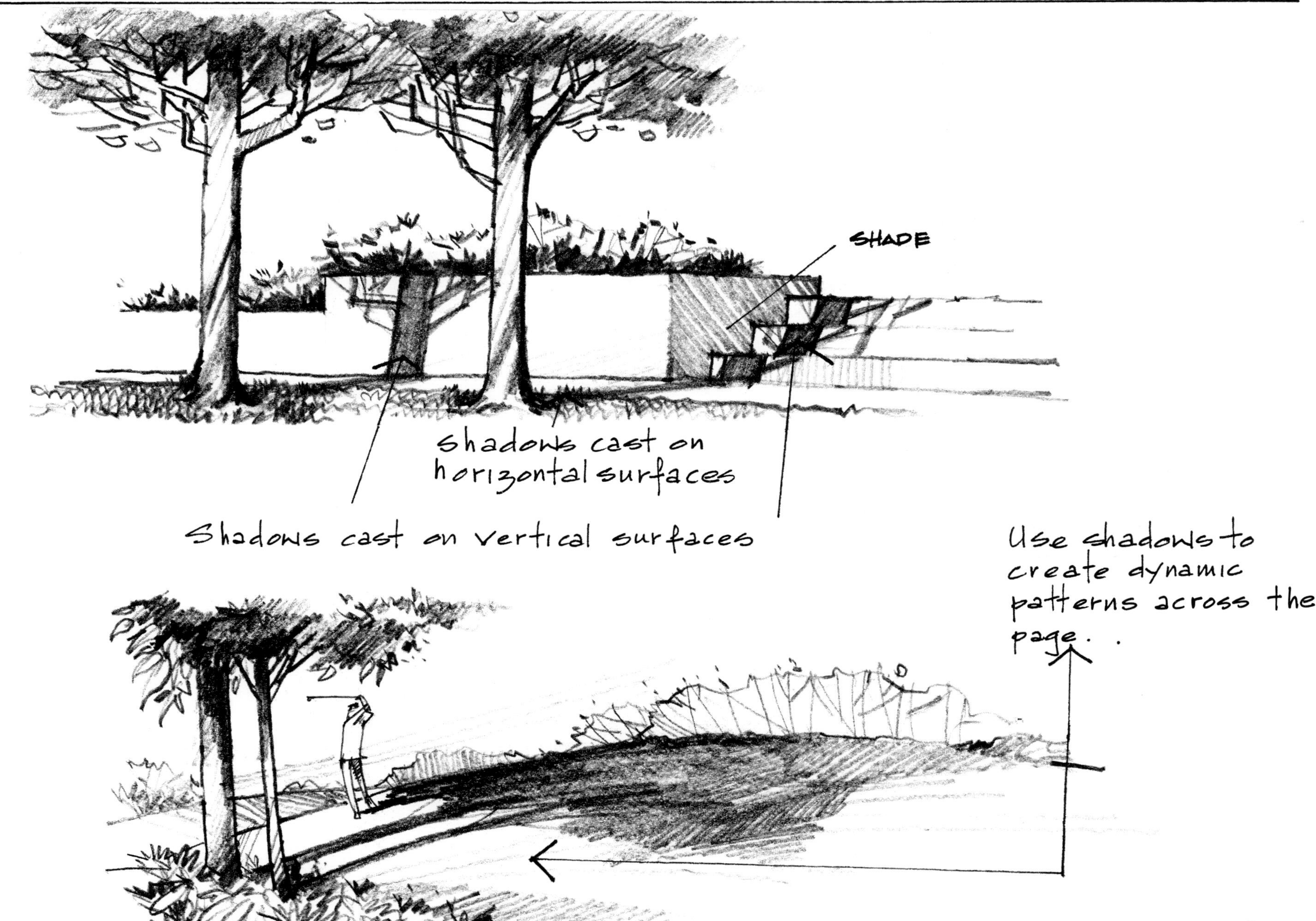
SHADE
shadows cast on horizontal surfaces
Shadows cast on vertical surfaces
Use shadows to create dynamic patterns across the page.

BUILDINGS

Transformation of a cube

Increase in: Complexity of planes
Complexity of dark & light contrast

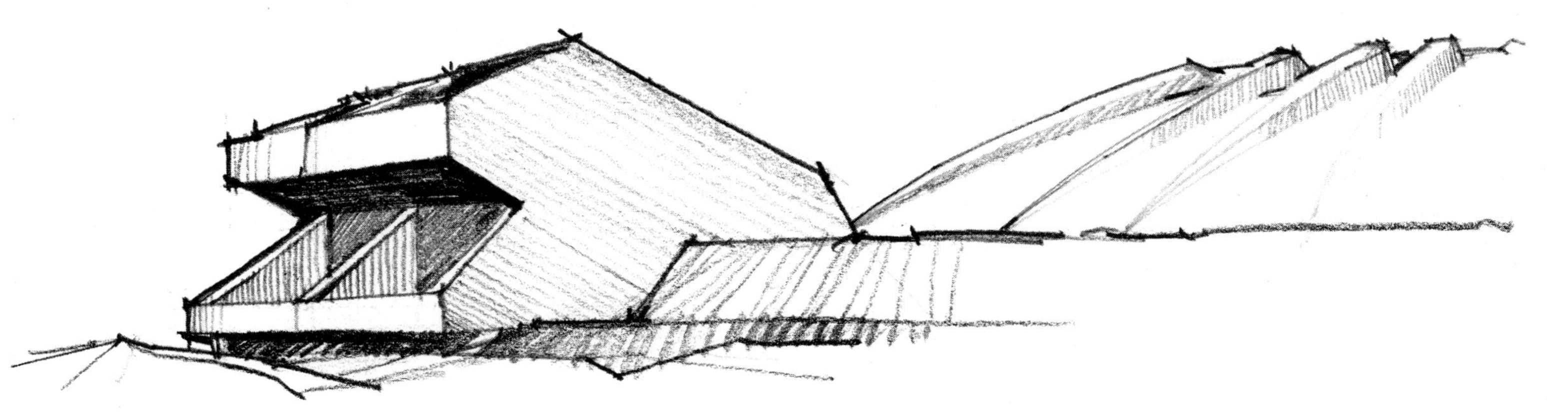

Forms become more complex.

Sun coming from top (to the left) at high angle behind building.

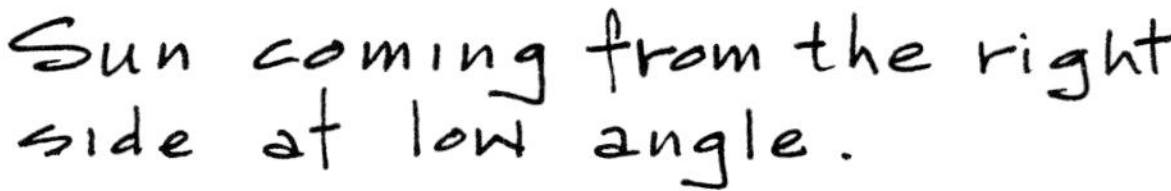

Sun coming from the right side at low angle.

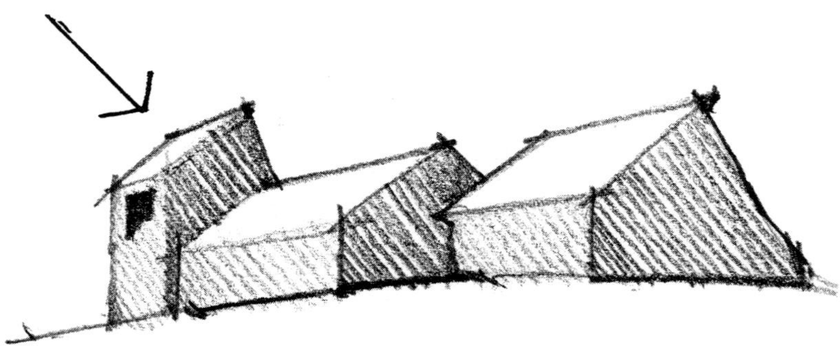

Sun coming from behind the building.

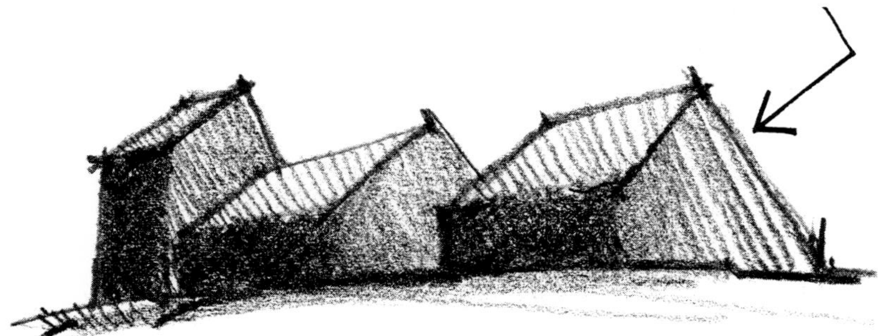

Sun coming from the front.

Building and landscape are both in sketchy, loose style.

Building: hardedge; detailed. landscape: softedge; loose.

An attempt to emphasize the architecture & downplay the landscape.

step: 1
- outline the building (basic form)
- adjust perspective
- locate all details (door / window)

step: 2
- outline the building with profile line
- observe sun's orientation
- shade the planes that are in shades
- staighten the lines

step: 3
- Refine shading
- clean up shading errors with a good eraser and erasing shield
- use a sharp pencil to touch up the edges and details
- add background and foreground

examples of touch-up

BROAD STROKES

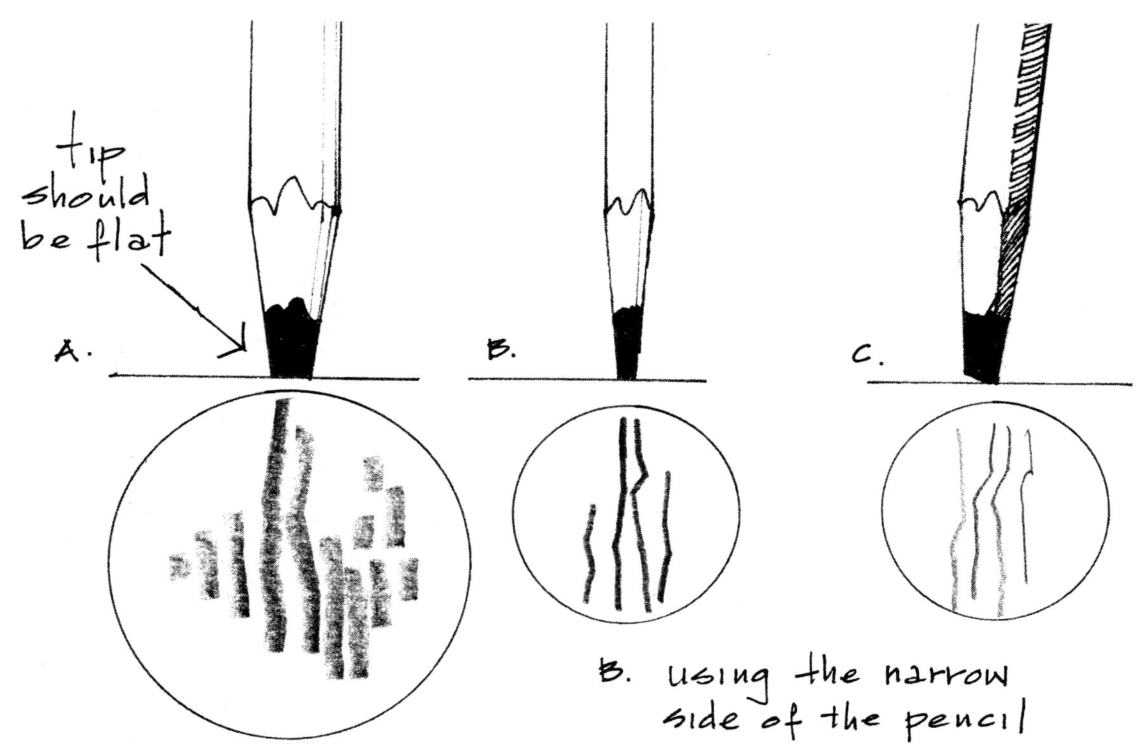

By holding the pencil at various angles (by rotating it), you can get a variety of line widths from this kind of sketching pencil.

B. using the narrow side of the pencil

C. holding the pencil sideways and using the corner of the tip.

A. using the broad side of the pencil.

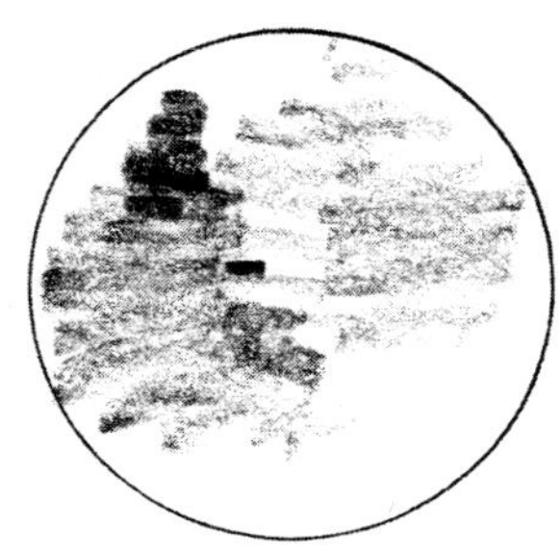

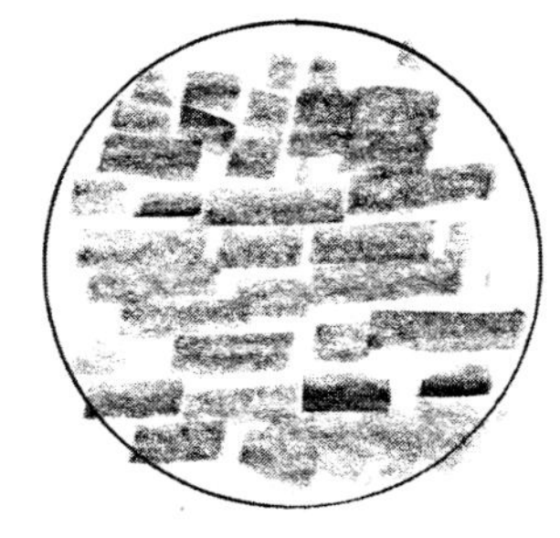

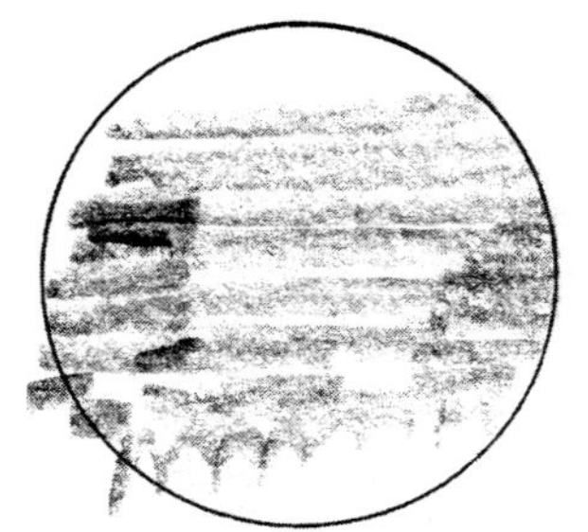

* Fundamental stroke exercises

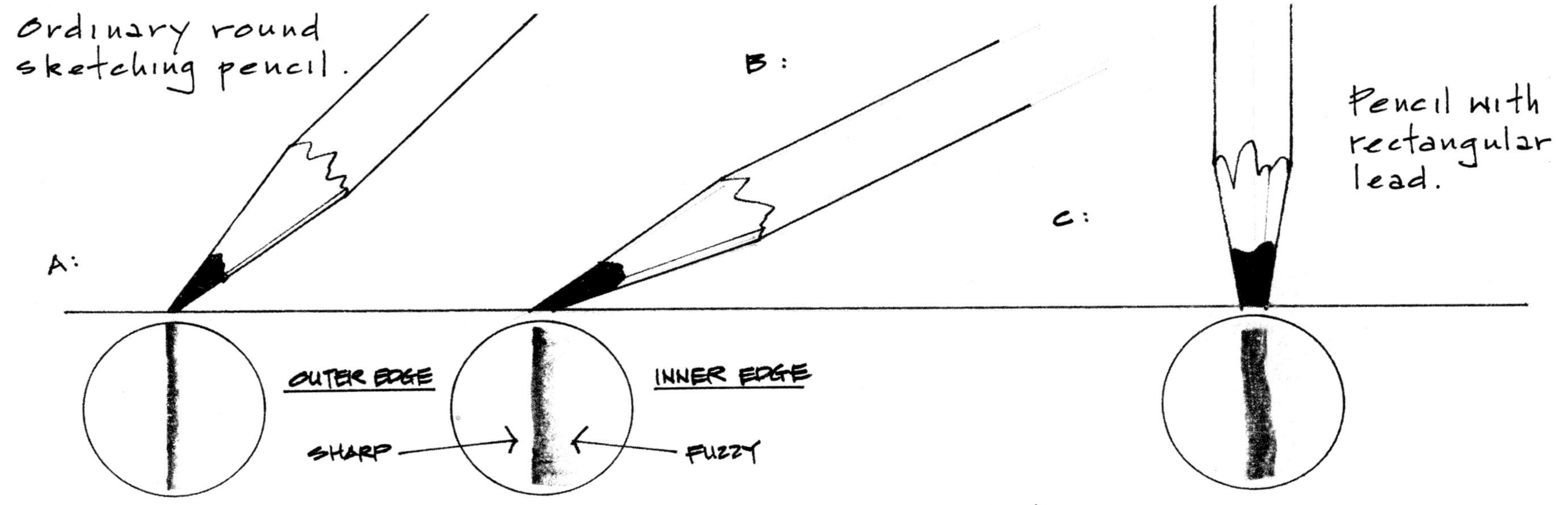

Comments:

It is difficult to maintain consistent line width unless your grip and pencil angle are also consistent.

The outer side of the line tends to be sharper than the inner side.

The width of the broad stroke depends on the angle at which you hold the pencil.

Comments:

The flat sketching pencil are slightly difficult to get used to, and they are not as flexible as ordinary round pencils.

The advantage of this kind of pencil is that one can maintain consistent line width and tone.

Of course, the width of the broad stroke depends on the width of the lead tip.

Tree shown with different styles of broad strokes

Broad strokes and tree trunks.

Use individual strokes (horizontal, vertical, or diagonal) for major structure; leave some white areas to indicate the roundness of tree trunk; use corners of the lead tip for fine branching structure.

Use flat sketching pencil as if you're painting with an oil painting brush.
The beauty of broad-stroke sketching is to reveal all strokes as they gradually build up the texture.
The sketch should be a composite of strokes in various widths instead of lines.

HUMAN FIGURES

Average adult

child

2y

y

x

1

5-6x

1.5

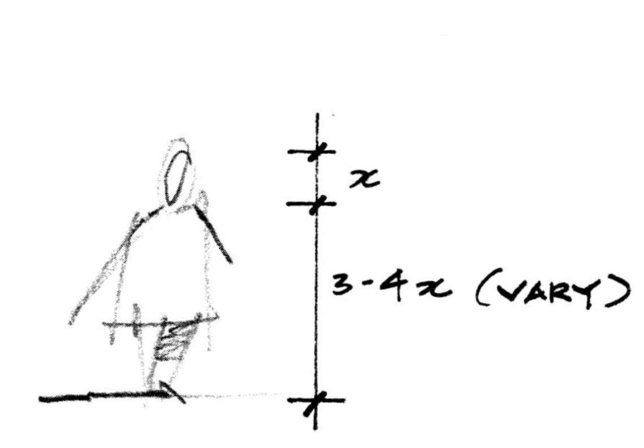

1. PROPORTION

note:

degree of detail should be relevant to the whole picture context (i.e. a rough, sketchy drawing will not work well with nicely drawn figures).

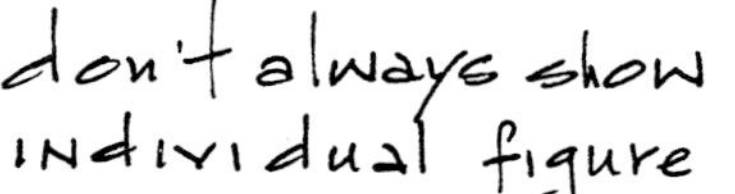

don't always show individual figure

show people engaged in talking

show back view as well as front

show them carrying things in their hands

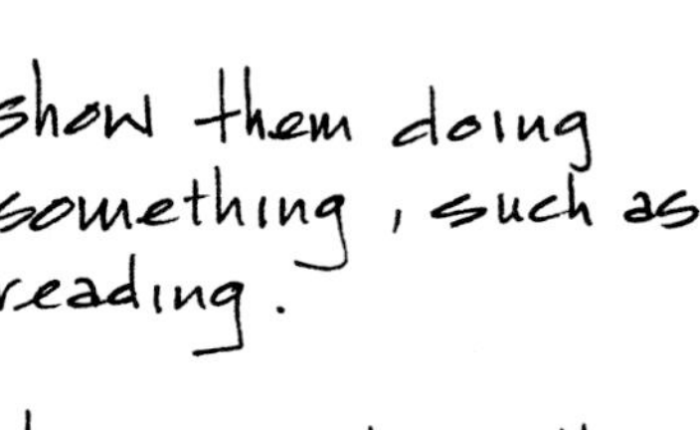

show them doing something, such as reading.

show people with gestures such as waving hands or hands in pocket.

show both sexes and kids. show children in action

show people walking dogs. pushing baby carts etc.

show background figures in groups

If design permits, show figures sitting, leaning against wall or sitting on top of wall.

All these suggest human relationships, friendship. they are realistic and make the people belong to the entire picture.

symbolic

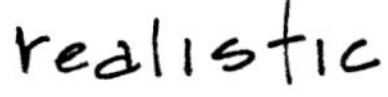

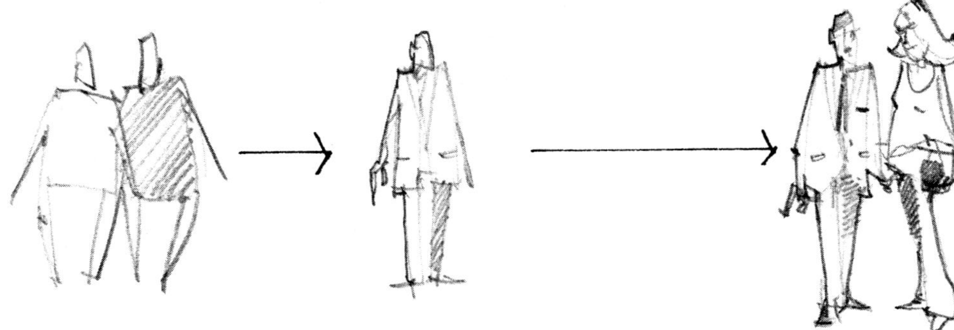

: used as scale indicator or for background

: not only used as scale indicator, it also humanizes the design by suggesting action, participation, as well as involvement.

Ocassionally, cartoonlike figures are good for a certain kind of sketch because they enhance the feeling of the drawing.

However, they should be used carefully so that they will not overpower the main theme of the drawing.

Use cartoonlike figures only when the subject matter is appropriate.

show figures dressed in contempory styles. Update your knowledge of fashions.

show a variety of characters.

Avoid oversized figures in foreground

Avoid abrupt change in the scale of figures. (from foreground to background or vice versa.)

Avoid showing action that flows beyond the page content (for example: taking picture that doesn't exist within the frame).

Relate figures to subject matter and content.

Relate figures to: locations.
time of day.
seasons.
race.
age groups etc.

step 1:
show outline.
proportion, and
gesture.

step 2:
refine outline.

step 3:
add details.

CARS

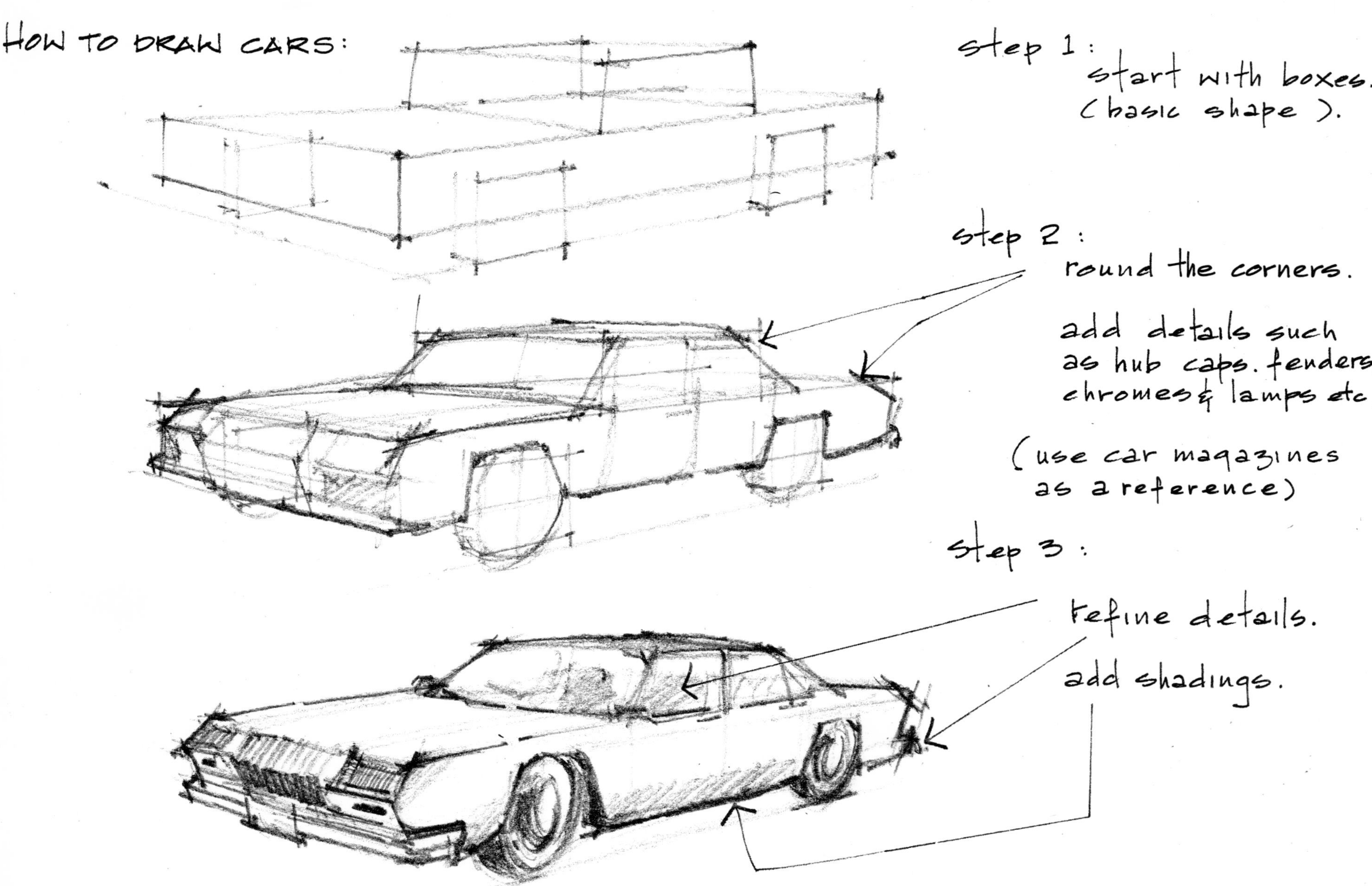
HOW TO DRAW CARS:
step 1:
start with boxes.
(basic shape).
step 2:
round the corners.
add details such as hub caps, fenders, chromes & lamps etc.
(use car magazines as a reference)
step 3:
refine details.
add shadings.

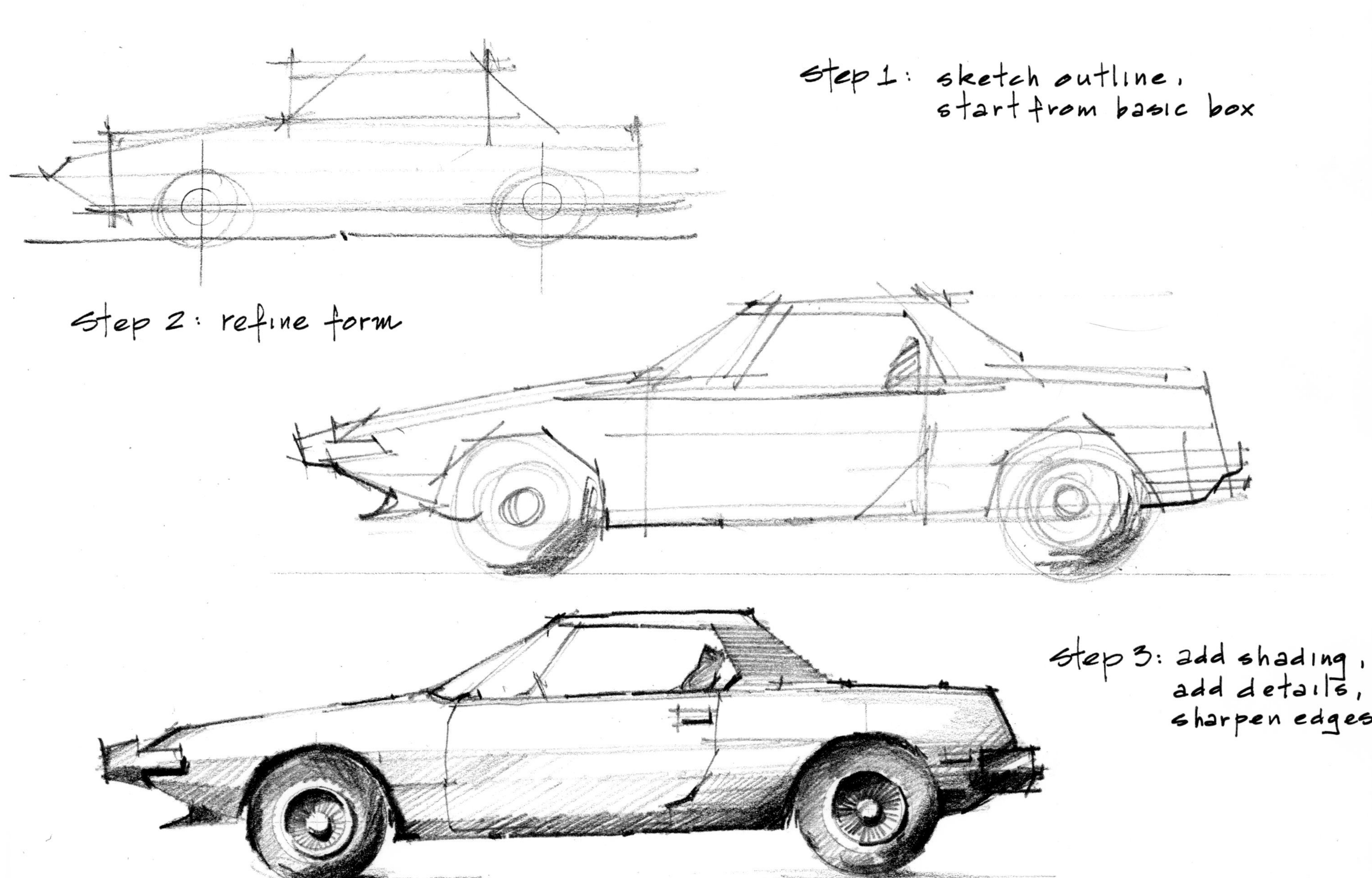
step 1: sketch outline,
start from basic box
step 2: refine form
step 3: add shading,
add details,
sharpen edges

CARS IN PERSPECTIVE

Different ways to show cars:

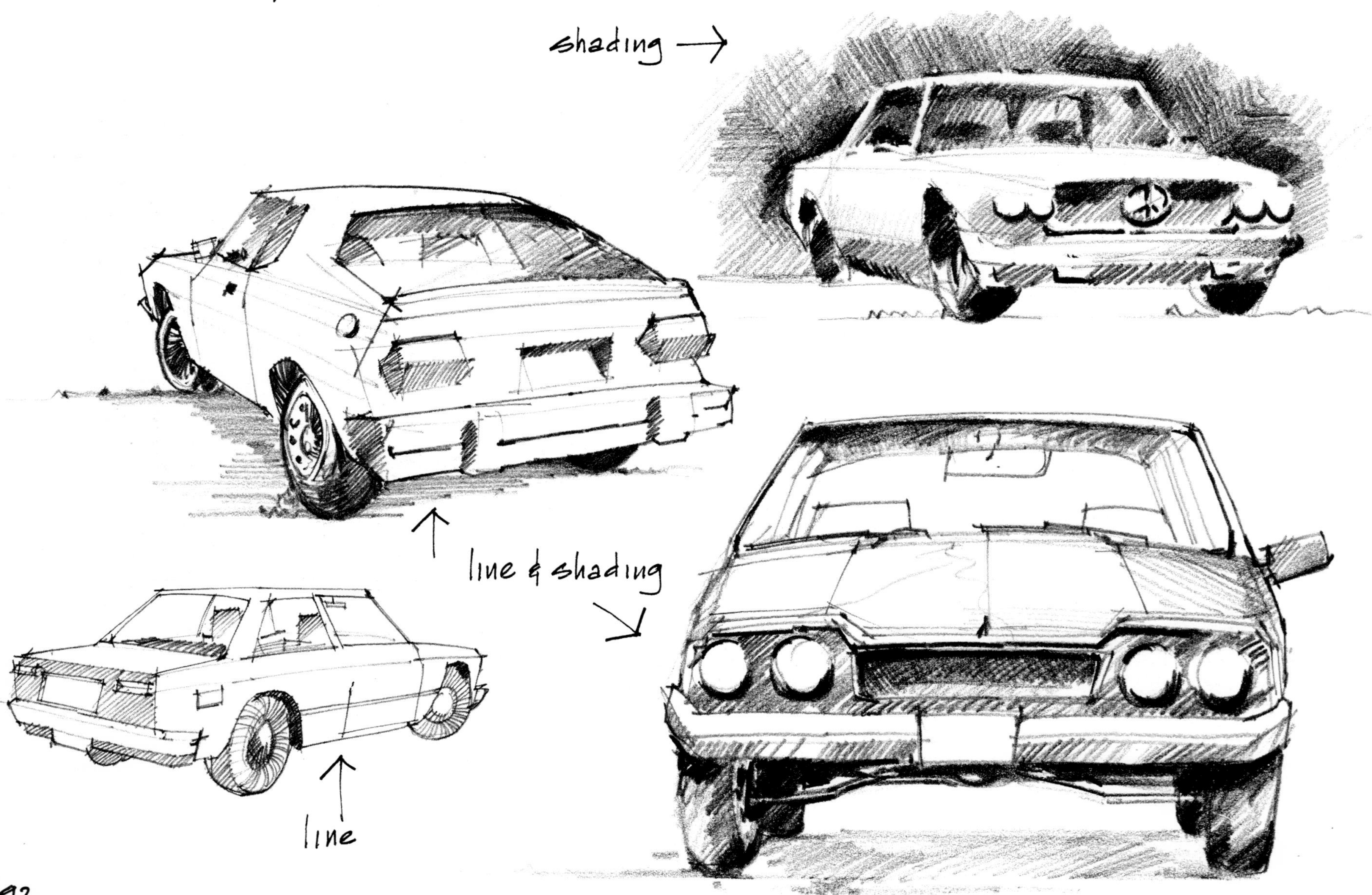

REFERENCE BOOKS

Black, Arthur. LANDSCAPE SKETCHING. New York, McGraw-Hill, 1950

Guptill, Arthur. PENCIL DRAWING. New York, Reinhold Publishing Corp., 1959

Kautzky, Ted. PENCIL BROADSIDES New York, Van Nostrand Reinhold, 1960

Kautzky, Ted. PENCIL PICTURES. New York, Reinhold Publishing Corp., 1947

Watson, Ernest. PENCIL SKETCHING - Book I, New York, Reinhold Publishing Corp., 1956

Watson, Ernest. THE ART OF PENCIL DRAWING. New York, Watson-Guptill Co., 1968

INDEX